What people are saying about

Laughing Again
A Survivor's Guide to Healing Depression

Roxanne's story is a ray of hope in the midst of staggering depression stats. For too long, the medical community has only pointed to psychotropic meds as the panacea for treating the depressed brain, but we do our clients a disservice when we don't share the powerful truth of Roxanne's 7 Rs for depression recovery and prevention. With a pastor's heart and a researcher's brain, Roxanne is, simply stated, The Real Deal. She has lived this journey, and she has the science to back up her claims. <u>Laughing Again</u> *is a must-read for those who struggle with depression, those who love them and the professionals who treat them.*

> Sally King, MSW, LCSW, LSCSW
> Tri-County Mental Health Services, Inc.

This is NOT just another 'depression self-help' book. <u>Laughing Again</u> *grabs a hold of your heart and soul; it has you at page one! It is as if you put on magic glasses that allow you to literally see and feel from the perspective of someone trapped in the treacherous world of depression.*

EVERY person who has ever had any amount of depression, sadness, fear, guilt or self-doubt, ever had any confusion about love, our purpose, how to forgive ourselves, how to forgive others, how to go on, how to heal, how to be happy, how to find joy or how to take life day by day NEEDS to read this!!

<u>Laughing Again</u> *will capture you at the deepest level. You will immediately begin reflecting on your own life and the choices you have made, the paths you have followed, and as you read on, you begin to see that all of it is divine order. You realize*

that YOU are very powerful, that YOU are indeed VERY connected to the Higher Intelligence that has created ALL!

There IS a greater plan for you, a greater purpose, and YOU are here to heal, to learn, to love and to live at MANY levels. This is a magical book that will take you on a magical journey, and in the end, you realize it is YOU who is the magician.

Roxanne, thank you! Thank you for opening your heart, sharing your soul and helping people to reconnect with who they really are: divine, powerful, loving, magical beings on an amazing journey we call LIFE!

Michael Brown, ND, AANP
Functional and Integrative Medicine Specialist
Co-Owner and Co-Founder, Wellness Dimensions

Roxanne's remarkable story shows that it's possible to overcome severe depression by changing one's thinking and living environment. Her recipe for healing exemplifies the power of combining thoughtful reflection, sleep, diet, exercise, breathing, light, laughter and love for long-term wellness. I highly recommend this exceptional book.

Farrel Douglas, MD
Neurologist
Private practice

Laughing Again

*A Survivor's Guide to
Healing Depression*

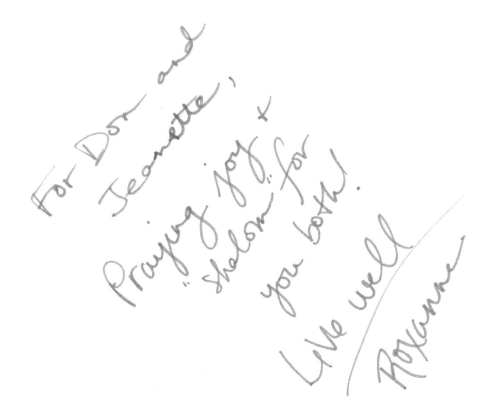

For Dot and
Jeanette,
Praying joy &
"shalom" for
you both.
Live well
Roxanne

Laughing Again

*A Survivor's Guide to
Healing Depression*

by Roxanne Reneé

Roxanne Reneé
www.RoxanneRenee.com

ISBN-10: 1453885013
ISBN-13: 9781453885017

Library of Congress Control Number: 2010915601

Printed in The United States of America

MEDICAL DISCLAIMER

Laughing Again: A Survivor's Guide to Healing Depression by Roxanne Reneé, all coaching and training offered by Roxanne Reneé, the *Secrets of Mental Mojo*™ seminar series, the *Living Beyond Depression*™ seminar series and all other seminars, articles, interviews, books, videos, audio books and web content developed by Roxanne Reneé are based upon her own research and experience of intentional, therapeutic, wellness lifestyle choices that support mental, physical, emotional, relational and spiritual health.

Roxanne Reneé is not a healthcare provider. This book is not a substitute for medical advice. All content including text, graphics, images and information available in this book is for general informational purposes only. The content is not intended to be a substitute for professional medical advice, diagnosis or treatment.

Do not rely on information from this book in place of seeking professional medical advice. Do not disregard professional medical advice or delay in seeking it because of something you have read in this book. You are encouraged to confer with your doctor or healthcare provider with regard to information contained in this book and related materials.

Roxanne Reneé is not liable. Roxanne Reneé does not assume responsibility for the accuracy or appropriateness of any advice, course of treatment, diagnosis or any other information, service or product discussed in this book. Your use of or reliance upon any information in this book is solely at your own risk.

Your continued use of this book will be deemed a consent to this disclaimer and a waiver of any claims you may have against Roxanne Reneé for reliance upon her materials, including this book, any adaptations, articles, interviews, audio content, video content, web content and seminars.

DEDICATION

To all who suffer the hell of clinical depression—

you are not alone.

There is hope.

I'll hold on to it for you until

you can carry it again for yourself.

Contents

PART III
7 Secrets to Live Well Today

Foreword

Depression is a tragic illness. It robs its victims of their energy, their memory, their joy, their confidence, their restorative sleep, their concentration and their ability to love, work and play. The World Health Organization now labels depression as the single leading source of disability on the planet. It is also one of the most deadly, accounting for nearly one million deaths each year via depression-linked suicide.

As a clinical researcher, I've worked for two decades to eradicate this treacherous disease. It's been a long battle, one marked in turns by daunting setbacks and thrilling break-throughs. Along the way, I've had the good fortune to encounter kindred spirits like Roxanne Reneé who share the passionate desire to help others escape the suffocating vice-grip of depressive illness. What sets Roxanne apart from most other clinicians, however, is the fact that she has *experienced firsthand* the process of healing from depression—she has lived the road to recovery, and she understands it in a way that only one who has battled the disorder on a day-to-day basis can. As a result, she speaks with the quiet, convincing authority of one who has been there, and I know her story will prove to be a source of inspiration and hope for many who have long since given up on any possibility of a return to health and wholeness.

Remarkably, Roxanne discovered many of the key steps to recovery on her own. By paying close attention to her body's cues and by poring through the published research on topics like exercise, diet, sunlight, sleep, social connection and negative thinking, she was able to fashion for herself a tailored program for sustained recovery that is quite similar in several respects to the Therapeutic Lifestyle Change (TLC) program that my research group has developed and clinically tested over the past five years at the University of Kansas. In fact, when Roxanne first contacted me a few years ago after learning of my treatment research, I was struck by the genuine excitement in her voice over the fact that a clinical researcher like me was willing and able to confirm her own intuition that *changing the way we live can have a profound effect in changing depressive brain chemistry, and can far exceed the effects of simply swallowing a pill.*

Since that first meeting, Roxanne has been an invaluable source of encouragement in the ongoing development of Therapeutic Lifestyle Change. More importantly, she has tirelessly promoted a lifestyle-based approach to the treatment of depression through her engaging lectures, workshops and writing. Her voice rings with the authenticity of someone who has been to Hell and back, and her heart is filled with compassion for the millions who remain to be rescued. I am privileged to know her, and I have no doubt that her readers will find comfort, illumination and invaluable guidance in the pages that follow.

Stephen S. Ilardi, Ph.D.
University of Kansas, Lawrence

NOTE TO THE READER

Clinical depression has a way of messing with the mind. My memories of events may be skewed; this is my subjective experience. I have done my best to communicate clearly and accurately. I have changed some names and certain details to protect the privacy of family, friends and acquaintances. Any errors are unintentional, and they are solely my own.

Laughing Again

A Survivor's Guide to
Healing Depression

PART I

Memoirs of Madness

❧ 1 ❧
Suicide Note

September 16, 2000

My dearest, dearest sons—

I love you so much. Tonight, we had your 3-year birthday celebration. So many people were here. There are so many people who love you, and I know, whatever should happen to me, that you will always be surrounded by much love.

Mommy is very sick. She got sick physically, but that's not all that's wrong with Mommy. Mommy's heart is broken, beyond repair. It has nothing to do with you; you did not break Mommy's heart. You are amazing and wonderful and full of joy and delight.

I am devastated that I cannot be part of the family with your daddy that you deserve, the family I dreamed we would be. I am so sorry I failed you, my dear sons, so sorry. I know you will never understand this, but I hope that one day you will forgive me.

And know, too, that if God is as merciful as I've been taught and as I've always believed, I will watch your incredible lives unfold from Heaven, and one day we will be reunited in a place where there is no brokenness, no depression, no abandonment...only joy.

You deserve a better mommy. At least I helped to bring you here and to this point, and even at three, you are amazing. You are such blessings. I got to have a big role in that. I adore you, but I've really messed up my own life.

You can heal, my loves. I believe in you. I will always believe in you. You are strong and wondrous, and your lives will bless many people. I am honored that I got to meet and to know you, even for this too-short time.

I know you love me, and I'll take that love with me. My love will remain with you, in your heart and in every cell of your body, though you may never consciously remember me. Love is strong as death.

I love you,

Mommy

❧ 2 ❧

Journey into Darkness

I didn't wake up one morning and suddenly decide to kill myself. No, that decision was reached incrementally. Day by day, I sank deeper and deeper into the heavy muck of a terrible despair. It was a devastating journey through profound darkness that lasted four, excruciating years. My darkness was clinical depression. My survival is grace.

I'm not so very different from each of you. My story is not unique. In fact, you may see parts of your own life or the life of someone you know or love reflected in my story. According to the National Institute of Mental Health, the facts are clear:

- 1 in 4 Americans will experience an episode of clinical depression in their lifetime, and the number is rising.
- Suicide rates are rising in every age range.
- Clinical depression is currently the second most costly disease in our society—with direct treatment, unnecessary medical care, lost productivity, lost work days and shortened life span costing over $92 billion every year—and the costs are rising.

- The World Health Organization ranks clinical depression as one of the leading causes of suffering and disability on our planet.

I am not alone. Depression is a global epidemic. I share my memories with you in this first section to provide a window into that darkness we call clinical depression. Some are my actual writings from that time, like the suicide note I wrote to my twin sons after their third birthday party or the excerpts from my journals. The rest is my attempt to describe an experience for which words are, quite simply, inadequate.

And yet, it is important to try. My purpose for this first section is two-fold: first, to help others currently in the dark wilderness of clinical depression feel less alone and second, to help those who love them gain a better understanding of their experience. As you read my story, please open your mind to the truth that if I can heal, and stay healed, so can anyone.

You don't get closer to death, without dying, than I did. My diagnosis was Major Clinical Depression, very severe, treatment-resistant, hand in hand with Panic and Anxiety Disorder, and Post-Traumatic Stress Disorder (PTSD). I was hospitalized four times during the year 2000 because I was actively suicidal from January 1 until December 28.

But how did I move from happy and healthy to treatment-resistant, suicidal depression? For me, ironically, it started with an answered prayer. After years of infertility, my husband and I were expecting—twins!

Throughout the summer of 1997, when I was put on strict bed rest from week 22 to week 36 of my twin pregnancy, I experienced significant lifestyle change in several important areas. I was not allowed to engage in any form of exercise. I had to be horizontal at all times, unless I was using the restroom. I showered sitting down. I ate in a recliner. I became a living incubator. Though I took excellent nutritional supplements based upon the knowledge I had at the time, I ate for comfort, which for me meant loads of sugar and unhealthy carbohydrates. I was indoors constantly because I was instructed to stay cool, calm and quiet.

I had almost no social connection because being around people made me happy, which lifted my energy, which raised my blood pressure, which endangered the babies. One time, during week 28 of my pregnancy, I was enjoying time with friends. I was so delighted to be around people that I allowed myself to laugh...and I went into labor. Later, at the hospital, I got this message: Don't laugh—you could kill the babies!

I lived with constant fight-or-flight energy, but I could not express it. I had to remain calm at all times. Don't laugh; you could kill the babies! Don't get angry; you could kill the babies! Don't feel anything that could raise your blood pressure; you could kill the babies! Don't mess up in any way; you could kill the babies!

Numerous times each day and night, I would take readings of a variety of bodily functions, and a machine would send this information to the doctors. Daily, a nurse would visit to monitor both the babies and me. My blood volume grew so high that the blood vessels significantly compressed the nerves in my wrists, resulting in severe carpal tunnel syndrome. Even holding a fork was excruciating. Though I practiced prayer and meditation and biofeedback, I lived with unrelenting pain and a constant underlying sense that at any minute all three of us could die. My relationship with my husband suffered as we both dealt with the terror of this time in strikingly different ways.

For brain function, it could be argued that the most crucial lifestyle change I experienced was ongoing sleep deprivation. Anyone who's been pregnant or who has known a pregnant woman understands that in the final month it is difficult to sleep. Your body is, quite simply, stretched to capacity. A full-term uterus measures around 40 centimeters. Mine hit full-term status at 22 weeks, obviously too early for the babies to be born. By the time of delivery, my uterus measured some 65 centimeters.

"Uncomfortable" cannot begin to describe the way my body felt. My abdominal skin stretched until it ached constantly and split from the pressure. My intestines were smashed to the sides and didn't function optimally, making digestion a painful process. My spleen was twisted around and behind. My liver and stomach pushed into my lungs, making it impossible to breathe deeply. I would not take painkillers or sleeping pills because I did not want to introduce any chemicals that could hurt the babies. I slept fitfully, in very small doses.

Finally, after 14 weeks of bed rest, on day one of week 36, my babies were born. Because they were premature, they spent time in the neonatal intensive care unit. Initially they had some special needs, and they required round-the-clock, focused care. I was committed to breast-feeding, and they needed to nurse every two hours. This meant I slept in 15-minute intervals, between feedings. Further, though we worked with lactation consultants, the babies were never able to nurse properly, and this caused me significant pain and tissue damage.

My body simply could not withstand the constant sleep deprivation and the relentless pain, and my blood pressure rose so high that my kidneys were in danger of shutting down. So when the twins were six weeks old, under uncompromising doctor's orders, I stopped breastfeeding in order to get more rest and to heal. The babies immediately developed colic, and for the next 3 months they screamed in agony from 10 p.m. to 3 a.m., no matter what we did. I did not get one solid night's sleep for over eight months.

All this resulted in a frustrating phenomenon—my brain ceased to function as I had always known it to function. It was surreal. If thoughts were train cars on a track in my head, it was like the track had huge chunks missing, and it was like the train cars were traveling in a thick fog, a fog the consistency of tapioca pudding...or maybe swampy marshland. I could not think clearly. I seemed to watch things from a distance, perplexed by my brain's inability to function properly, disconnected from the people around me and sometimes even from my own feelings.

I was chronically exhausted. I was sad a lot. I was angry a lot. Less and less was enjoyable to me. More and more, life felt overwhelming, and eventually there was this oppressive heaviness that descended upon me, making it hard to move, hard to even breathe. I knew that I was in trouble by the time my twin sons were six months old, and I took myself to see a medical doctor and a psychotherapist. I started counseling. I began taking anti-depressants. Some made me numb. Some made me worse. Sometimes the side effects were simply intolerable.

Things continued to deteriorate. My marriage imploded, and by the time my babies were 18 months old, their father and I were living in separate bedrooms and actively pursuing divorce. Though I was deeply hurt for many years at the way my husband abandoned me when I most needed his support, now I try to look at him with compassion. How terrifying it must have been for him to watch me slowly disintegrate, completely helpless to fix me. I was not the only one to suffer the effects of clinical depression. Those who loved me dealt with their own kind of pain and fear.

In the spring of 1998, my father died. Though this man had not reared me, had not been my "daddy," he was nonetheless an important part of my life, and I grieved the loss. Over the following months, I began to wrap my sadness about me and snuggle into it like a blanket. It didn't feel good, but it felt comfortable in a way, familiar.

In desperation, I made unhealthy choices. One such relationship choice turned abusive, and this led me into deeper and deeper isolation. I left my job as a pastor because I felt profoundly guilty and completely incompetent. I grew to hate myself. I lost 50 pounds because I lost all interest in eating. I hurt everywhere, all the time. The physical pain was relentless, and no treatment could alleviate my symptoms.

Grief upon grief, loss upon loss mingled with the slow disintegration of my integrity, living in the shadow land of deceit where secrets, lies and guilt poisoned my soul, I came to detest myself. Depression, born out of the amazing and chaotic dance of pregnancy-induced lifestyle changes, grew in the turbulent strife of a dying marriage. It festered and spread in the chronic exhaustion of single parenthood. It gained strength in the prison of isolation demanded by a dark love affair. It became a torturous monster with its own will, a monster that fed upon rage, rationalizations and abuses both subtle and devastating. Despair and anxiety became my constant companions.

I became convinced that I could never heal, that my spirit had already left my body, never to return. I became convinced that physical death was the only means by which I could escape the unending physical, mental, emotional and spiritual pain. I became convinced that death was a gift of protection I could offer those I loved, that my children would be safe from the pain and horror living inside me if I were dead.

This, of course, is not true. Had I completed suicide, my children and those close to me would have been much more likely to take their own lives one day. I would have cursed them had I completed suicide, but I was convinced that I was a source of darkness in their lives and that they would be better, safer, happier if I were dead and gone. How twisted is the logic of depression.

To offer you a window into the experience of clinical depression, into the way that a depressed brain thinks, I share with you selected excerpts from my journals during those painful years. I have deliberately chosen not to go into narrative detail about the events surrounding these entries, though you will likely be able to deduce certain specific circumstances of my life as you read them. Were I to write the full story of those years, I would need another book, and my intent is not autobiographical. Rather, I hope that the thoughts and feelings I share here reveal the universal themes and patterns of a mind stuck in depression. In places, these journal entries are quite raw. I left them that way on purpose, to accurately document the experience. I apologize in advance should any of my reflections cause unnecessary pain.

Laughing Again - Roxanne Reneé

❧ 3 ❧
Journal Excerpts

February 1998

Some days I feel like I'm just barely holding it together. I know I am strong, but I can't seem to find the strength, the clarity. I'm so indecisive. I have a hard time thinking, like there is a haze in my head. I'm tired. I feel overwhelmed. Insecure. What the hell am I doing? Should I be doing ministry? I feel intimidated. What happened to my center?

I want to run away, to hide. I'm operating in a constant mode of anxiety, and I don't know how to break the pattern. For instance, I'm anxious that one of the babies will cry. Why? I know what I will do if they cry; I will take care of them. But, I'm always holding my breath and clenching my teeth. Their cries plunge into my soul like knives. And there are two of them, only one of me. I'm not enough. It is such an awful feeling to be holding one sweet baby and listening to the other wail because he, too, needs you, and you cannot go to him. You cannot be fully present for both, it seems.

Some days I wonder what God was thinking. Am I fit to mother? I love my babies so much. I would never, ever give them back even if I could. But this has really rocked my world. I don't know how to be now. I know I am taking great care of them, but I do not feel like myself. My adrenals are on overdrive, in constant fight-or-flight to keep me functioning at all. I am so tired, always tired.

Oh God, rebuild me, my shaken spirit, my weary body. Bring me home to myself again. Renew my hopes and heal my body. When I don't understand, make me to trust you and to live both with and in the mystery.

If you hear and care for the baby ravens when they cry, surely you hear my babies' cries. God, I cannot be enough, but you are. Soothe their souls and bodies; be a balm to them. They know you; surround them with your Spirit. Help me to trust.

August 1998

I'm wearing my sunglasses today, to hide the pain in my eyes, but you are not fooled. When we meet, you sense the ache in my soul, and your spirit moves toward me. You ask, "Are you okay?" I pause for a moment before I answer, weighing my desire to be truthful with you against my desire not to impose.

The truth is I feel like I'm dying inside. My heart is broken. The heaviness, the pain, makes it hard to breathe. And, by the way, sometimes I cannot stop shaking.

Last night, it was real to me again. He was holding my wrists against the bed. I could feel his strength, and I could feel my weakness. I was fighting, but I could not break his hold. Then I could feel him hurting me, deep inside me, hurting. Why am I not numb anymore? I wanted it to stop. I didn't want to remember.

Was it a dream? No. It was not a dream because I was awake, lying in the fetal position and still hurting. Skin burning, bleeding, uterus and ovaries cramping, breasts bruised. It hurts. I wanted to vomit. I wanted to run away. I can't believe it can still hurt this much after all these years. I'm starting to feel angry. Don't want to deal with this, walk through this, fight this, feel this, look at this ugliness, weakness, shame, guilt, fear, pain. But I must, because to be whole I must integrate this grief.

All these things race through my mind, my soul, before I answer. I decide the parking lot at Wal-Mart is not the proper place for this kind of honesty regarding recent date rape flashbacks.

It is so hot outside, and it's your day off, your time. No one really wants to listen to, look at, this kind of hurt when it's this hot outside. So, I force a smile and say, "I'm fine," but you know I'm lying. So do I.

December 1998

I'm just sick, sick in my heart, sick in my soul, becoming sick in my body. How did I get to this "me," this life? Motherhood is not what I expected. I love my boys. Yet, caring for them is overwhelming. I'm not alone. I have help and support, but there is this weight, this responsibility, this 24-hour-a-day caring and planning and administrating and nurturing and it's endless...endless. There are no breaks. Even when I leave to do something away from them, they are still with me. I feel drained. I cannot sustain the endless needing. I'm not endless. I'm acutely aware of my finitude. I feel used, used up. I thought this role would bring me such joy. Why do I feel like I'm dying inside?

My marriage—oh God, I loved him so much. Now, I'm just numb or angry. My heart is not with him. I remember. I remember how happy we were, days when I would count my blessings from the moment I awakened until I fell asleep. I find no joy in "us" anymore, no peace, no connection. I look at him and feel no attraction. God forgive me, at times I have wished him dead. Then, I shudder. This man, with whom I chose to share my life, where did we go wrong? Can it be fixed? Do I want it to be fixed? He adores our children. I feel lost. Funny, I've been fighting so I don't lose myself, and I'm lost anyway.

And in my wandering lost-ness, where it is mostly twilight, I grasp at anything that feels like life, like light, like hope. I followed my heart, against my training, and found some happiness, found love. Yet, it's tainted, for I love one who is not free to be mine, and I am not free to be his. The joy we share when we are together is shadowed because we cannot be honest about our love. I was not created for lying. I am no longer a person of integrity. I cannot remain a pastor without integrity.

Sometimes, in moments of paranoia, I wonder if it's all a set-up. I wonder if this situation has not been engineered or at least assisted by the powers of darkness to make me ineffective. They must be celebrating their good fortune. I spend so much time in misery that I have little time left for God's work. Satan doesn't wear horns for me. No, my temptation is handsome, strong, intelligent, fun, gifted, sensual, vulnerable, alive. Is he my soul mate? Is he a demon? Is he simply a human being who I was called to love in a holy way, but failed because I fell in love with him? I dreamed I left my marriage for him. I lost my pastorate, many friends. I broke apart my children's home, and then as I came to him to be embraced, he pulled off his face, a mask, to reveal a demon, laughing, mocking me. "Gotcha." Is that paranoia or intuition? He would be hurt to know I even pondered such things, I think.

Nothing is going to happen to fix this. No one can save me. I must step up. My life. My decisions. Want out of the muck? Get out, then. How? End all contact with forbidden love? Leave my marriage? Is there another alternative? Is it possible to accept what is today, without changes, and be content with that? I've sure as hell been trying, and most days I fail.

My heart is breaking, breaking, breaking. Heaviness. Hurts to breathe. Oh God, when will this stop? What must I do? How much sadness until I break under the weight?

Laughing Again - Roxanne Reneé

January 1999

I've realized that I would always rather feel guilty than helpless.

I am tired. Tired of fighting, of believing, of sustaining, of hoping, of enduring, of encouraging, of forgiving. I want to run away, hide, curl up and nurse my wounds. Decide how to start over, discover who I am. Who am I? Be honest again.

How would I be different, how would my life be different, if I defined myself by my best moments rather than my worst?

Laughing Again - Roxanne Reneé

PART I: Journal Excepts

February 1999

I've been reflecting a lot lately on who I am—what I believe, what I have believed, my needs and desires, the life I have built, my motivations. Over the past five years, my perspectives have broadened. Maybe I'm finally growing up emotionally. I don't know.

I have always tried to be "good," to do the "right" thing. Achievement has always been connected in my soul to acceptance and love. Mom's threats of insanity or suicide if I ever left or ever messed up helped me to believe that love was conditional. Losing a parent is terrifying to a child, so I was highly motivated. I did everything for my mother's love and to insure her health. I developed into an excellent caretaker, denying my own needs from a young age so that I could give to others. Of course, this makes me well loved, but it does not make me healthy or balanced. I am surrounded by people who are used to having me give to them. When I try to give to myself, I meet resistance. If I follow through, I create chaos. Chaos is terrifying to me, too.

Things felt so crazy when I was growing up. I craved stability and orderliness, so I created my own vision of good/bad, right/wrong, how life "should" be lived. I delineated things very clearly. Church played an important role in my mind-set; religion helped me to define the boundaries. Everything was cut and dried, and I set off to build my life according to the guidelines I had determined. The problem is, having very successfully built a "perfect" life according to my guidelines, I find that my vision does not fit who I am and who I am becoming. It's like a box that once felt safe but now feels like a prison.

Here I am now, at age 30, and I have everything I ever thought I wanted: a husband, a great job that allows me a lot of time at home, two beautiful children, a house in the suburbs, friends, great vacations. You know, the life I looked at from the outside as a child and thought, "that's happiness." Only, now that I'm here and have worked so hard to create all this, I'm miserable because it's not me. It's mundane and monotonous and safe and pretty and boring and stifling and not real life. It's like a pretty world created to hide away from real life, from real pain. I don't want to hide in suburbia; I don't like it here. Maybe I'm not created to be this kind of mom?

Laughing Again - Roxanne Reneé

April 1999

At my father's funeral, I wear my sadness like a cape, and I ponder death. There we sat, the four of us, my step-mom and two siblings, in the front row. We sat and held hands so tight our bones made imprints upon each other's skin, connected in life, connected in grief. Flesh and blood and love, family; this man braided us together. There we sat, so small, so frail and weak against the backdrop of the inevitable unknown, daring to believe that death is not the ultimate separation. We sat and stared into the abyss, and faith pulsed between us like a heart beat — ridiculous, illogical, real, strong, filling us with power to live on.

Laughing Again - Roxanne Reneé

September 1999

I am in process, and it is hard work. It is movement, letting go and going on past the "fairy tale" dream. I still have a family, changed but present. I can still know parenting, love, commitment, stress, pain, fear, courage, joy...I can rebuild my integrity. I am growing stronger. I am learning. In darkness, faith still grows. As I reach out, I build new community. Grieve the old; make room for the new. Forgiveness makes me un-stuck. There is a new path for me now.

Laughing Again - Roxanne Reneé

January 2000

I can. I can beat this. I can know joy again. I can heal. Heal me, Lord. Remove this resistance that has rooted itself deep within my being, this resistance that weighs so heavily and refuses movement toward any person or activity that beckons me to step toward LIFE.

God, I ache. I am deeply despairing. Like the Psalmist, my tears have become my food; day and night I cry. I cry out for someone to save me, and though there are those who long to do just that, it is impossible. None can save me but you. None can save me but me. The depression, it's like a prison. No, it's like heavy, iron chains are wrapped around me, more and more chains, and they pull me deeper into the darkness, into the abyss from where there is no escape, no return.

I can see all that there is that is good, that is reason to live, and I fight. I fight because I have known richness and joy, because I want to rear my boys, because I have hope of having a life partner again, of experiencing love and health and even laughter again. But, it is so difficult.

The battle I fight is within, and Death has disguised himself as peace. He beckons me, "Come. Stop fighting. Rest. No pain here, only sweet release."

I don't want to die. Please, God, help me find the strength and courage to live, to fight this depression, to overcome. Be my strength. Sustain me, in Jesus' name.

Early February 2000

*Something is fundamentally wrong with me.
I am in despair, and I have never been more
unhappy in my life. Perhaps I made the wrong
choice. I thought I was miserable before—I
had no idea what misery felt like. I am either
actively thinking about self-destruction,
passively being self-destructive or running
away to hide. I sleep as often as I can. I
escape through reading and sleeping.*

*What brings me joy? My children, when I am
not completely overwhelmed. My friends, very
occasionally. My lover, mixed with pain.
Actually, I'd settle for just plain comfort
right now. Joy seems completely out of
reach. I feel so desperate for comfort and
help, I even reached out to my boys' father.
There was a time when we were very happy. I
miss feeling happy and blessed. I miss fun
and playful friendship times. I miss having an
in-house co-parent. I hate living alone, making
decisions alone, sleeping alone. I miss having a
job that felt profoundly meaningful.*

*Last night, I sat in the garage for a long time,
debating whether to just close the door and*

turn on my engine. What stopped me? The faces of my two, beautiful sons passed before my eyes. I love them! I cannot leave them. I want to share their lives. So, I went inside and wept and wept, called their father and wept and wept, actually invited him to bring the boys over and have all of us spend the night together. Not sex. Not reunion. Just simply the comfort of presence.

I am so tired of dread, hopelessness, weariness. I miss meals and hardly feel the hunger. Where and how did everything go wrong? I once thought I had the perfect life. Was it all just an illusion? A fairy tale? I almost don't care. I thought I wanted reality and depth. Now, I'd almost give...sometimes I just want it back so badly. Just erase the past few years. But that would mean no children, and losing them is too high a price to pay. I grieve and grieve. Feeling so sad and sorry for myself when really I have so much: food, shelter, transportation, two healthy, beautiful, wonderful sons, a steady job, enough income to get by, some people who truly care about me, access to medical care...

Even music, which used to be my most pure and powerful expression of emotion, brings me pain, physical heartache. I don't know where I'm going, and I hate where I am. I'm supposed to what, make PEACE with that?!

Laughing Again - Roxanne Reneé

Mid-February 2000

There are no words for my pain, but I must write anyway. Choose. Choose life. Choose, Roxanne. Choose, damn it! Choose life. Decide where you want to go and then say GOODBYE to the past. If you really don't want to go back then really leave. You can no longer exist in this middle area; it's going to kill you. Choose one or the other, and get moving.

I thought I had chosen. When I said I would leave everything I had, everything I knew, I had no idea how that would feel, what it would look like. It would have been easier, better for healing, to make a clean break. Instead, I stand with one foot, still, in each world: the world I made with my husband, and the world in which I am nothing I had planned to be. I married, I thought, forever. I was a wife. I built friendships, I thought, that were unshakeable. I was a friend. I was called to professional ministry. I studied. I served. I was ordained. I made a difference. I had an incredible job, one I found meaningful and life giving. I was a pastor. I built a life with my husband. I was a member of a growing community, one where I felt safe. I had a "home," not just a house, but a place in this world. Then, we had the babies, and I was a mom, a mom of twins. So, there it was: wife, friend, pastor, community member, mom. Looks so perfect. Should have been, but it wasn't. I have a hard time remembering that it wasn't perfect lately.

If it was so perfect, why the seeking of a relationship with a man, a relationship of more depth, more connection, in a way that my husband and I did not have? Was it unconscious, the longing? My will was set to be happy with what I had, what I'd built, what I always thought was "happiness." Yet underneath there bubbled something, something that sought expression, something fundamentally a part of the "who" that I am.

Now, there are those who would call this "something" of which I speak "sin," or "rebellion" perhaps. And if that is so, then every move I have made since acknowledging that "something" has been destructive, the work of evil, and I have been in opposition to God. The pain and isolation and devastation I now live are the results of my sin. "The wages of sin is death," death in the here-and-now.

And the way back to life is repentance, returning back to all I was and all I had, and forever fighting against, squelching, that "something" in me.

Only, there is no going back. I suppose there could be reunion with my ex-husband, but we both would have to want that. I don't think I could fall in love with him again. There is so much about him that I do not find attractive. He lacks substance and depth. I do not find him strong, or heroic, or brilliant or loyal. I appreciate the way he shared homemaking. I appreciate his playful energy with the kids... but he left me when I needed him most.

If I reject the paradigm that the "something" in me is rebellion or sin, then what is it? Is it that part of my self that has outgrown the paradigms of my youth? Is it my Wise Woman, my experiential self? Is it the Roxanne who seeks existence and expression beyond the box-become-prison of safe, suburban dream life and traditional believing? And if so, where the hell is she now? If SHE reached out for new and different life, then where is her strength and faith during this hell-time of transition? Where is her courage and vision and confidence and power?

I am sick to death of being sick unto death. I am sick of my tears. I am sick of feeling powerless, of feeling overwhelmed. I am tired of grief. I cannot embrace my present or my future while willingly remaining chained to my past and to ideas I have outgrown. I must recreate my paradigm. I must rebuild. I am certainly capable. Where do I want to go? Who do I want to be?

March 2000

I did this. I did it. Me. I created this situation, with help of course, but I am responsible for fucking up my life. Or maybe one day I will say "transforming" my life. I ran from the pain of guilt into a worse pain—isolation.

The time has come to say goodbye to an entire way of life, to a dream, a goal I've worked toward for over half my life. No wonder I feel lost. Today, I offered to try to mend my marriage. I was refused. I left that relationship too quickly, and I had to know, moving forward, that I was willing to try to repair it. But, it takes two. Now, I can walk away knowing that there is nothing more I can ever do to "fix" us, and that knowledge though painful sets me free.
It is over, really over, and I can close this chapter in my life to begin another.

My husband, perhaps you loved me as deeply as you could, and you certainly hurt me deeply as well. I know I hurt you, too. I choose today to take the good with me. I will remain connected to that love and joy as

I watch our boys grow and celebrate their lives. They were conceived in love. They were desperately desired. They are adored.

I also know today that I must forgive the bad. I do not condone your sin against me. I do not —I will no longer —allow myself to look upon it as punishment for my own sin. You fucked up. You made bad choices. I gave you opportunity to draw close to me, and you refused. You devastated my soul. You would not celebrate me, my growth. You would not honor my needs. I am not powerful enough to force you to do the things you did, make the choices you made. I did not force you to seek out love and comfort in the arms of another. You caused this divorce as much as, if not more so, that I did. So, I absolve myself of YOUR guilt. I will no longer carry it around and whip myself with it. I am only responsible for my own mistakes. I am only responsible for my own guilt, my own betrayal, not yours, never yours. There is no more I can do to make amends for your sin.

God, forgive me. Roxanne, forgive yourself. I choose to forgive you. I choose to forgive me. I move forward with hope of renewed and profound connection with my Creator. I move forward with hope of a future that could be wondrous and fulfilling beyond the grasp of my imagination. I am set free to love another with a clear conscience over my past, to love myself with a clear conscience. Goodbye, husband. Goodbye, life of my 20s. Goodbye dream. In letting you go, I open myself to a new dream; I make room for a new thing.

Come then, grief. You, who I've fought, kicking and screaming and run away from at all costs, come. I must move through you to get to a place of peace and healing. I seek wholeness, and I must dance with you, grief, to move on. Come. You are not so strong. I am a child of God, and there is strength available to me that can withstand your wretched devastation. I choose to live. I choose to remember who I am. Dance with me, then, you son of a bitch. Dance and feel your power wane. I accept your presence. I accept my reality. I am divorced. I am sad. I am single. I am okay. I am going to shine again. I am a great mom. I am strong and wise. I do know. I will act on what I know.

Psalm 116:1-4

I love the LORD, for he heard my voice;
    he heard my cry for mercy.
Because he turned his ear to me,
    I will call on him as long as I live.
The cords of death entangled me,
    the anguish of the grave came upon me;
    I was overcome by trouble and sorrow.
Then I called on the name of the LORD:
    "O LORD, save me!"

Mid-April 2000

I feel lost and frightened and small and not enough, defeated, angry. I have not always been this way. I have known myself to be strong, competent, passionate, fun, intelligent, creative...a fighter. What happened to that woman? I need her now.

I want to move beyond this place of darkness and pain and loneliness and despair. I lost my marriage and my dream of family and many friends and my home and my vocation and my church and my way of life and my sense of alright-ness and my sense of who I am and my sense of feeling safe. Everything upon which I built my life is gone, and I'm un-connected. With the severity of this depression, I may lose custody of my children, too.

I experience very little joy. Depression is so exhausting, and frankly it is boring. I am tired of such intense misery and such intense focus upon my misery. I want to move on and heal, not just bury the pain. I'm stuck in guilt and grief over yesterday and in anxiety, no terror, and the overwhelming-ness of today.

What happens if I let go of the fairy tale dream? I gave up on having my own happy childhood long ago. I promised myself I would get to experience the "happy" of childhood from the other side, by making sure I gave my own kids a happy childhood. If I let this go, if I accept my failure, do I give up my last link to the dream of knowing in some way a happy childhood? Can I accept the fact that life isn't always going to happen according to my terms?

I feel so guilty. I have punished myself by leaving professional ministry. I have punished myself by remaining stuck in my misery. I have punished myself by refusing to forgive myself, by refusing to accept God's forgiveness. Like God can and will only forgive AFTER the sin ends. I have been completely de-constructing. If I don't stop now and start reconstructing, I will lose my children; I will lose my very life.

I want to choose life. I want to forgive myself. I want to accept grace, to live within grace. I want to get unstuck from my misery. I want to let go of the past. I want to dwell in wholeness in the present. I want to move toward a future with hope. I need to accept forgiveness.

My mother said, in effect, "Make me happy, or I'll kill myself or go insane." I am saying, in effect, "Make me happy, self, or I will kill you or go insane." How long will I reenact this dynamic that threatens my very existence?

There is no Scriptural evidence that God doesn't forgive sinners. In fact, the reverse is true. The Bible is filled with stories of God loving and chasing after sinners, like me. God wants me, still, yes especially still, to contribute to what is good in this world. God will use me in spite of and because of my self.

I don't know how to live in a state of grace. How ridiculous. This is the lesson, is it not? I must learn not only to proclaim grace but to KNOW grace, to experience accepting it. I guess before this I never really thought I needed saving. Now, I do.

Laughing Again - Roxanne Reneé

PART I: Journal Excepts

Late April 2000

It's hopeless. I will always be this way, this sad, this alone. I will never be married to my soul mate. I will never be "me" again. That happy, passionate, creative, loving, wonderful girl seems dead. She will never be resurrected. God seems gone forever. I cannot trust me. I've made too many mistakes to fix. I hate me. I hate my ex-husband. I hate my situation. I suck as a parent. I suck as a person. No one could like me or love me. I am pitiful. There is no way out without losing custody of my babies. Where is my savior? There is no savior. God cannot use someone as broken as me in ministry. I am a death-bringer. I am dying. I am killing me. I deserve only to suffer for my sin. The punishment is eternal. There is no grace for me. There shall be no friends for me. I am not worthy of love or friendship. I cannot fix what is broken in me, in life. I will doom my children if they stay with me or know me at all. I am not the good parent. I cannot survive alone. I am disconnected. I lost my ability to survive. I will never laugh again. I am stupid. I am never going to recover. I am always going to be angry.

Laughing Again - Roxanne Reneé

Mid-June 2000

I am angry that there is no plan. I don't have a plan. I want a plan. I feel so sick, so angry, so scared. There is no freedom. Stomach in knots, worst feeling, walled up heart. Like no one can help me. Like I made a bad decision. I can't live this way. Have to get through my wall. Hurts when people touch me, hurts.

My babies, my babies, my babies, my babies, my babies. It's wrong for a mom to self-destruct. For anyone. Why, God, did you let me get to this place? Pain. Panic. Pain. Panic. I hate this fear. I hate this weakness. I hate this pain, this anger. What if I can't be fixed?

Dark, writhing pain beyond words. My babies. My babies. Oh God, Oh God, my babies, my babies, my babies...I'm separated from my babies. No one can understand. I'm so angry it has come to this. I have not been able to successfully deal with my own pain, and now their father's home is their only home. I hate myself for that.

I have guilt over abandonment, not being the primary custodial parent, falling apart, divorce, sin, weakness, being unable to provide for my children's needs, failure, failure, failure. I can go no further.

Battle or no, their father has been caring for the boys, and the paperwork just makes current reality complete. I can argue no more options. I'm tired, no, exhausted. I have "what-if'd" about daycare and jobs and medicines and doctors and where to live and hospital versus no, and I have no peace, no clarity. All I know is he is taking care of the boys, and I am not.

I'm not taking care of me, either. I can't pull inside much further without disappearing completely. I keep telling myself to engage — engage life! Yet I keep withdrawing. It's too much. The pain is too much.

Late June 2000

My heart has been dead, my eyes blinded, my spirit bound. You, Oh God, can raise the dead, as you did Lazarus. You, Oh God, can give sight to the blind, as you did the man blind from birth. You, Oh God, can break the chains of oppression and depression, as you did for the Gerasene.

I have been so angry that life didn't turn out right, not remembering that it's not over yet. I'm at my end, and I'm ready for your new beginning, God. It was you who called and ordained me. It is you who promise to heal and strengthen me to do whatever I must, regarding all aspects of my life: children, relationships, work, home, joy. It is impossible to go back as I am, but not as a new creature, in your power and surrendered in faith to your way.

Psalm 51:1-17

Have mercy on me, O God,
  according to your unfailing love;
According to your great compassion
  blot out my transgressions.
Wash away all my iniquity
  and cleanse me from my sin.
For I know my transgressions,
  and my sin is always before me.
Against you, you only, have I sinned
  and done what is evil in your sight,
    so that you are proved right when you speak
    and justified when you judge.
Surely I was sinful at birth,
  sinful from the time my mother conceived me.
You desire truth in the innermost being;
  you teach me wisdom in the inmost place.
Cleanse me with hyssop, and I will be clean;
  wash me, and I will be whiter than snow.
Let me hear joy and gladness;
  let the bones you have crushed rejoice.
Hide your face from my sins
  and blot out all my iniquity.
Create in me a clean heart, O God,
  and renew a steadfast spirit within me.
Do not cast me from your presence
  or take your Holy Spirit from me.
Restore to me the joy of your salvation
  and grant me a willing spirit, to sustain me.
Then I will teach transgressors your ways,
  and sinners will turn back to you.

Save me from bloodguilt, O God,
    the God who saves me,
    and my tongue will sing of your righteousness.
O Lord, open my lips,
    and my mouth will declare your praise.
You do not delight in sacrifice, or I would bring it;
    you do not take pleasure in burnt offerings.
The sacrifice acceptable to God is a broken spirit;
    a broken and contrite heart,
    O God, you will not despise.

Laughing Again - Roxanne Reneé

Mid-July 2000

I'm scared I'm freaked out I cannot cope I don't know how I'll pull it all together the job the living situation the custody oh my God oh my God why have you forsaken me I am alone my husband stopped loving me because I am unlovable I suck I am a loser I lost it I am so anxious I am so panic-filled I want peace and assurance Where are you, God? I cannot continue I cannot continue I cannot utilize help I need someone to take care of me no one can take care of me I want a mommy I want to live with family and my boys I want to be done with this phase everything will explode

I hate myself I hate God I hate my life I've ruined everything I cannot be forgiven don't deserve it will never be happy again I don't deserve any peace I don't deserve any friends I've screwed up beyond repair I hate everything I am a fuck up I am incompetent I cannot be a minister I am so weak I suck I am so angry that I've brought things to this place I am so angry there is no quick fix of course it's been almost a year since my

divorce so that's not a quick fix in my book
why does God seem so far away why is there
no peace why is life so hard and shitty why
can't I seem to pull together I'm a failure I
have lost all that is good about me I deserve
to suffer because I betrayed my vows I
deserve to suffer I suffer I am judge and
jury and have condemned myself to
deconstruct I don't deserve my sons I am
not worth such wonder and beauty in the
face of my awfulness

Late July 2000

Waves of anxiety, nausea, roll over me, no
sleep, angst, heat, shakes, tingling arms. I
invited it said do your best (instead of fighting
it and trying to remain calm) Go! Go! What
are you trying to tell me? What? Alone does
not = bad. Why the terror I've been laying here
having a panic attack for an hour nearly,
started after I laid down. Just want to rest,
so much adrenaline. Tired, so tired. Head
hurts. Want to sleep or have headache gone.
No luck. Chemicals. Chemicals. Chemicals.
Where am I? Words of wisdom, need
thoughts of wisdom. Help me, God. What's
the panic saying? I'm safe. I'm safe right
now. Can rest, watch movie, journal, whatever
needed, take a walk, why so tired? Take a walk
around the block? Watch a movie? What what
what? Feeling frantic. Want to hide, to sleep
but the panic. What? Walk? Okay, walked a
few blocks better better somewhat

Laughing Again - Roxanne Reneé

August 5, 2000

Isaiah 43:18-19

> Forget the former things;
>> Do not dwell on the past.
> See, I am doing a new thing!
>> Now it springs up; do you not perceive it?
> I am making a way in the desert
>> And streams in the wasteland.

Today, when I woke up, my first thought was NOT related to death. I walked. I ate breakfast. I drove myself. I didn't do it on time, but I did it. I have gained six pounds. I am here to bring out God-light, God-colors, God-flavors in the world. I cannot help others heal in the future if I don't walk this path. I'm pissed that I must do this, really angry. But, I don't get to change certain parts of my reality. It sucks, but I must not give in to suicide. I can bear this with God's help and friends' help and family's help. I am still the same person. I'm traumatized, but I'm still "me."

Laughing Again - Roxanne Reneé

August 12, 2000

Psalm 27

The LORD is my light and my salvation—
    whom shall I fear?
The LORD is the stronghold of my life—
    of whom shall I be afraid?

When evil men advance against me
    to devour my flesh,
When my enemies and my foes attack me,
    they will stumble and fall.

Though a host encamp against me,
    My heart will not fear;
Though war arise against me,
    In spite of this I shall be confident.

One thing I ask of the LORD,
    this is what I seek:
That I may dwell in the house of the LORD
    all the days of my life,
To behold the beauty of the LORD
    And to meditate in His temple.

For in the day of trouble
    he will keep me safe in his dwelling;
He will hide me in the shelter of his tabernacle
    and set me high upon a rock.

Then my head will be exalted
    above the enemies who surround me;
At his tabernacle will I sacrifice with
    shouts of joy;
I will sing and make music to the LORD.

Hear my voice when I call, O LORD;
    be merciful to me and answer me.

My heart says of you, "Seek his face!"
    Your face, LORD, I will seek.

Do not hide your face from me,
Do not turn your servant away in anger;
    you have been my helper.
Do not reject me or forsake me,
    O God my Savior.

Though my father and mother forsake me,
    the LORD will receive me.

Teach me your way, O LORD;
    lead me in a straight path
    because of my oppressors.

Do not turn me over to the desire of my foes,
    for false witnesses rise up against me,
    breathing out violence.

I would have despaired unless I had believed
    that I would see the goodness of the LORD
    in the land of the living.

Wait for the LORD;
    be strong and let your heart take courage;
    wait for the LORD.

How can I survive? How can I do this? It's become pretty clear that I won't heal overnight. It hurts so bad; it all hurts so much. God is only giving me, well, not even strength for today. It's hour by hour at best. I am so angry. I am so lonely. I am so sad. I am missing so much of my sons' lives, missing so much time with them.

God has provided for me. Please, God, grant me the strength to get that job and to heal, to fight. I'll miss a hell of a lot more of their lives if I lose this battle. If I lose this battle, I really do lose everything.

Things to celebrate today: got out of bed, showered, ate, wrote in my journal, balanced my checkbook, organized my meds, got snuggles and hugs and kisses from my two beautiful sons who love me...my body is still somehow functioning, alive in spite of toxins, pain and depression...my friends...money to pay bills...my son lovingly stroking my hand, the exquisite sweetness of him

Laughing Again - Roxanne Reneé

August 13, 2000

Psalm 55:4-8

My heart is in anguish within me:
  And the terrors of death have fallen upon me.
Fearfulness and trembling come upon me,
  And horror has overwhelmed me.
And I said, Oh that I had wings like a dove!
  I would fly away, and be at rest.
Lo, I would flee far away,
  And live in the wilderness.
I would wait for him who will save me
  From my cowardice and from the storm.

The death feelings, depression feelings, are here and BIG. I promised I would go to church, and so I must. Then out to lunch. Then meet with him, he who brings me always closer to death. Where is the "up" and laughter from last night? God, I HATE the way it is lost over night. I can't seem to get organized. Every little task feels like too much. I need to leave in a few minutes, and I feel so shitty. Donna, who daily battles monsters so terrifying that I cannot even conceive, is in better spirits than I am. How is it that I'm not a fighter? Burn out. Want to lie down and die. It's truly crazy. I have so much for which to live, so much I could give. I hate this depression—HATE IT! How long, O Lord, how long?

Laughing Again - Roxanne Reneé

August 14, 2000

I have always been "outer" defined, attained value through doing (and doing exceptionally well). Now that I am not able to "do" well, now that I've FAILED—sinned, disintegrated, lost my job, home, marriage, custody, sanity—I have no value in my inner judge's eyes. I'm no longer Superwoman. I've become human, and I am not acceptable to my self, such self-loathing. No grace for me. Judge and jury within, sentence is death. I've usurped the role of God. I'm on the throne, judging self, meting out punishment. I have been so "good" in the past, salvation earned in my subconscious mind, arrogance, pride. Appears I was the Pharisee, confident in my goodness. Only now I am not good, and my judge offers no grace to me.

This depression is about me becoming human. If I refuse, I will die. I must become internally defined. Healing will be slow. My life is all tangled up. Once tangled, how is a skein of yarn untangled? With time, patience, determination, focus, the help of others and cutting.

According to John, these are my reasons to live:

1. If I die, the pain for my two little boys will just be beginning.

2. My friends and family would be unbearably sad and feel deeply betrayed.

3. It is possible to feel better.

4. God has more for me to do on Earth; my ministry is not yet completed.

5. My legacy is about life, not selfishness, cowardice and death.

6. There is more life that I want to experience.

But to heal, I cannot use my mind, my brain, which has always made me so competent. I have no blueprint for healing. I am forced to live taking baby steps in faith. I hate it! I am angry like a 3-year-old who can't have her way. I struggle. I am so stubborn. I refuse to commit to healing. I'll show everyone I am not strong. I'll show God that I cannot be forced to grow in adversity so I can be a better minister at some time in the far-distant future. FUCK THAT.

September 12, 2000

I am indeed a fool. I am 31 years old, and I am bound by the fears of a 12-year-old, the life design of a 17-year-old, and the choice of a 20-year-old. My parents divorced when I was 12, and I was left home alone a lot. I was terrified of being alone. I still am. At age 17, when different choices my mother made led to the devastation of our family, I promised myself I would be healed by doing marriage and family "right" one day (i.e. staying married). I am divorced. At age 20, I misguidedly believed that my chosen husband was capable of loving me the way I need to be loved. He is not; he never was.

I must face my fears and face the facts. I am capable of learning to live alone. I cannot be healed by any "perfect" situation outside me or by any person outside me, God included, so it seems. My ex was not willing to love me, and I must dream a new dream. I must love my self into wholeness.

O God, the pain, please let it leave. I must somehow move on. Please, please, move me on. God, are you even real? What in heaven's name is going on? What in hell's name? Is all this rambling supposed to work some miracle? I hurt, so bad. Maybe I should just quit.

Don't run, Roxanne. Please don't run. Stay and fight. Stay and survive. Stay and win.

September 28, 2000

*Abba, Father God, you gave me much love.
I had a good life. Take me now into your
kingdom. I believe that not even death can
separate me from your love. I believe.*

Laughing Again - Roxanne Reneé

Mid-October 2000

I cannot heal. Please, God, kill me. I beg you, daily, but you won't. Doty won't help me die; no one will. I fucked everything up. I want to die and go on to Heaven, to be forgiven, to run to the next place of living. No one will help me, and I'm too scared and incompetent to successfully complete any suicide attempt.

I hurt so bad I want to die. God forgive me, death feels like a good option. Heaven, or cessation of consciousness, even a "do-over" would be okay...would I be punished in the next life for all the pain I brought to my sons, my family, my friends? Would God show mercy?

It's like I'm resigned to death. My mind is set. Could I be otherwise? Resigned to forgive? Resigned to love myself? Resigned to hope? Resigned to heal? I used to love life so much. Where did that go?

I say I want to be healed, to be whole, but I fight tooth and nail against that which would heal me. It would be easier to die. I've become used to being sick. I'm scared to heal. How ridiculous, but it's true. I don't want to be alone, and being healed and whole means living alone and being okay. It is really true that I'd rather be sick than okay? What the fuck is wrong with me?

It's like I'm holding myself in sickness. My body needs to take a walk, but here I sit. My boys miss me, but here I sit. I could line up a job interview that could bring me back home, but here I sit. I'm a failing failure. I SUCK! Why won't God just take me home? Why?

Oh God, where are you? Why are you so far from my groaning? WHY WON'T YOU HEAL ME?! Help! Don't you want me to be well? Don't you want me to be there for my sons? If so, I need significant help. Big time, bigger than you have given already. I am sorry, God. I am sorry that I'm not strong. I'm sorry that I need more help. Oh God, my God, don't leave me. Don't leave. Heal me. I cannot bear the pain. Help. My babies, God. Help. Help. Help. Please help.

I'm so scared. I think I'm more scared than I am hurt. Is that even possible? I can't even crack open the door inside myself to

look at the pain; it's too great. Could my
fear of the pain be bigger than the reality?
The fear is incapacitating. The fear makes me
incompetent. The fear started last spring.
The fear became anxiety then panic. The fear
undid me. Is it not the pain but the fear
that I must face?

Are you big enough, God? Are you strong
enough to help me face the pain and live
through the fear, alone, back in Kansas City,
over the holidays and beyond? What must I
do? Can I even do my own laundry and cook
and shop and clean and work and live, just
live? I am in terror.

My time is running shorter and shorter. Most
of my family has already given me up. Most
of my friends, too. They don't know what
else to do. Me neither. No more hope. No
more help. Suicide.

What the fuck happened to me, God? I am not
who I was. I am not who you created me to
be. I am not who I have the potential to be. I
have—Oh my God, it is true—become defined
by my shame, pain, terror, disease and sin. It's
not for lack of love, encouragement, money,
etc. You have reached out. I remain stuck.

Psalm 63

O God, you are my God;
    earnestly I seek you.
My soul thirsts for you;
    my body longs for you
In a dry and weary land
    where there is no water.
I have seen you in the sanctuary,
    and beheld your power and your glory.
Because your love is better than life,
    my lips will glorify you.
I will praise you as long as I live,
    and in your name I will lift up my hands.
My soul will be satisfied
    as with the richest of foods;
With singing lips my mouth will praise you.

On my bed I remember you;
    I think of you through the watches of the night.
Because you are my help,
    I sing in the shadow of your wings.
My soul clings to you;
    your right hand upholds me.
They who seek my life will be destroyed;
    they will go down to the depths of the earth.
They will be given over to the sword
    and become food for jackals.
But the king will rejoice in God;
    all who swear by God's name will praise him,
    while the mouths of liars will be silenced.

Late October 2000

You suck, God; you fucking suck. You said, "I will never leave you or forsake you," BUT YOU DID! Oh yes, I sinned. I know. But you allowed that to separate us as much as I did. Your people have shown me so much love, but what I need is an inside job. I need YOU to change my heart, or at least help me to change it. Yet there you sit, up in your heaven, so distant, so cold.

I NEED YOU! I have needed you for so long. I have begged and pleaded. Where are you? I need you inside my heart, inside my head. I CAN'T DO THIS WITHOUT YOU, AND YOU ARE NOT HELPING! Fuck. Fuck. Fuck. If you are so powerful, strike me dead right now. Yea, I thought so, you IMPOTENT, WORTHLESS DIETY!

I called. I cried out. I begged. I humbled myself. I've separated from my sin. I need you. Please help me. If you are capable but choose no action, you have a real dark side, you asshole. Asshole. Asshole. Asshole. Those Old Testament stories are bullshit, or else you'd be consistent. Fuck you. All I want is to be whole, healed, to serve YOU as a pastor, to live the life I've been called to live, BUT YOU WON'T FUCKING HELP ME!

How am I supposed to be a witness to your love when I don't feel it for myself? What the fuck else do you want from me? I've lost everything. Almost. What else? How long until you help on the inside? I FUCKING HATE YOU, AND I HATE ME MORE.

November 2000

I'm not even sure why I'm writing. It doesn't seem to change things. Last week, I saw my boys—so much joy, but bittersweet because I knew I had to leave them again. Oh God, my sons hurt. This hurts them so. It's devastating for me, their pain. They deserve a mommy who can be there consistently. I want to be that mommy.

Please grant us all a second chance. Please make me okay. Take me back to them in the next week or two. Lead me to employment. Lead me through healing, and for their sakes, God, make it happen in KC.

I adore them, Lord. Give me the strength to do WHATEVER IT TAKES. I know I won't be reunited with their father, and I know I may never marry again. I know you can make me okay living alone, and I know you can heal me—us—all of us.

God, take me back to KC, soon, and work out my healing there. I may not get a church position. Okay. Let me have one of the other positions. Make me new, God; do whatever is needed.

Just please, please don't make my sons have to hurt anymore. Please, take me back and give me the strength to make it, for them. That is all. Healing...for them, for me. Please, my Abba, please.

PART II

From Hell to Healing

❧ 1 ❧

Giving Up

Suicide ideation begins very subtly. My initial thought was "I cannot bear to take one more breath. I don't want to live like this anymore." In the beginning, I didn't want to die; I just wanted to stop the unbearable suffering. The pain was so great; to this day, it's indescribable.

I began to think fleetingly about dying, imagining for a split second just driving my car off a bridge, for example. Then, more and more, I would fantasize about dying as a means of escape—escape from the excruciating pain, escape from the relentless anxiety, escape from an abusive relationship and, in my mind, as a way to protect my children from darkness and from harm, a way for them to escape *me*.

I researched ways to kill myself. I developed numerous plans, and then I attempted to enact those plans. The first three times that I was hospitalized during the year 2000 did not heal my depression, but they did serve to keep me alive until mid-December, when I was hospitalized for the fourth time.

Laughing Again - Roxanne Reneé

❧ 2 ❧

Getting to Brookhaven

The drive from Kansas City, Missouri to Tulsa, Oklahoma is usually a benign and boring four-and-a-half hours, but the day a man drove me to be admitted to Brookhaven Specialty Hospital, that drive was an all-out war. The weather was brutal. It was sleeting so hard that sections of the highway were shut down, and occasionally he had to stop to scrape thick ice from the windshield. The cold seeped into my bones regardless of how high the heater was running.

I was so desperate to die that I contemplated jumping out of the moving vehicle into the mess of speeding and skidding traffic all around us. Aware of my state of mind, the man reminded me regularly that he had brought rope and was willing to literally tie me to the truck should I make the slightest move to act upon my dark desire.

I remember that I started spewing venomous words at him at one point, a few hours into the trip. Strangely, in the midst of this diatribe I spoke of myself in third-person. It was as if the voice and the words were being said "of" me but not "by" me. I remember internally observing this phenomenon with mild, dispassionate curiosity. The voice coming from me was filled with hate, and it said, "Give up and let her go. It's too late for her. She is already lost to you."

He confidently rebuked me, or rather he rebuked the voice coming from me as though it were demonic. Then, he demanded that I not speak. I remember internally thinking that this was ridiculous—he thinks that there is something demonic happening, and he thinks, what, that now I won't be able to speak? Seriously?!

In my mind, I heard my own disbelieving laughter. I thought, "Screw that! Now I'm going to say whatever I want." I opened my mouth to speak and found, to my profound amazement, that I was unable to utter a single word. After awhile, I lay down on the seat, and I did not speak at all for the remaining hours of the drive.

It was late at night when we arrived in Tulsa. When we pulled into the hospital parking lot, I became frantic. I did not want to be admitted. In a full-blown panic, I was struggling to breathe. My so-called friend agreed to find himself a hotel room first, then admit me to the hospital a bit later, giving me time to calm down.

As we sat in his hotel room, he began to kiss me. He said that if we had sex, I could stay that night with him in the hotel. I was desperate to avoid the hospital; I would have done anything he asked of me. Anything. So I did.

The next morning, he drove me straight to the hospital. As we moved through the long, paperwork-intensive process of my admission to the psych unit, I ping-ponged between feeling crushing despair and feeling completely numb. I much preferred numb.

When it was time for him to leave, he walked down a long hallway toward double doors that led outside the unit. I ran after him, crying, begging him not to leave me there. I reached to hold on to him, and hospital orderlies restrained my arms, dragging me backwards. I fought them, kicking and clawing.

He walked away. The doors closed behind him, and the electronic locks clicked securely in place. I ran to the doors and beat at them, screaming and crying, "Don't leave me here! Please come back. Please don't do this. Please. Please. Please." He never looked back, not even once.

Laughing Again - Roxanne Reneé

3

A Communal Shrug

I was sitting alone at a table in the cafeteria, picking at the first meal of this hospitalization, really just moving the food around the plate. I had been without an appetite for so long that I really could not remember what it felt like to hunger, to enjoy food's texture or taste, or to be consciously aware that a full belly satisfied more than the body. I was so committed to death that an act as basic to life as eating a meal seemed a betrayal of my ultimate desire.

Without warning, without preamble, a man sat down next to me. He was a tall, burly, blue-collar type with calloused hands and rough speech and a heart as big as the state of Texas. He said, "I don't know what could have happened to make such a pretty girl so sad, but I'm not leaving this hospital until you get better." And though I did not believe him at that moment, time would ultimately prove his promise true: Steve was eventually given the choice to be discharged earlier than I was, to return home and spend Christmas with his family, yet he chose to stay in the hospital, and to stay by my side as a voice of gentle encouragement, until the day I was sent home.

Steve introduced himself and told me a bit about his own struggle with bipolar disorder (BPD). He had been admitted that same day for a much-needed medication adjustment. He told me about his job, his family, the everyday details of his life. He asked me questions about my life, to which I mostly gave monosyllabic answers, if I answered at all.

Steve introduced me to other patients: Ted, a local fire station chief who also dealt with BPD; Dan, a Native American brought from the prison to the hospital for addiction treatment; Kit, a social worker whose entire life had disintegrated in the midst of her addiction to cocaine; and Cali, a talented Christian musician battling PTSD, depression, addiction and cutting.

Immediately and without reservation, they adopted me into their circle of friendship. With no reason I could fathom and no reward in it that I could see, these strangers befriended me. Individually, they sought me out and talked to me. They told me their stories. They asked about my story, and they did not stop asking in spite of my silence.

In groups and in one on one encounters, they encouraged me to fight to heal myself. They reminded me of my reasons to live. They stopped by my room on the way to group sessions, and if they could coax me to get out of bed they walked with me to class. They sat with me during meals. They explained hospital procedures and staff personalities. They schooled me on the ins and outs of life in this particular mental institution. They were kind to me.

When I told her of my plan to complete suicide at the hospital so that my family would not have to clean up the mess and asked for her help to carry out my plan, it was Kit who went to the director of the hospital and told him my intention. This won me a personal session with the director, who was a gifted and compassionate counselor and a former pastor, a session that was painfully humiliating and simultaneously powerfully nurturing, like being called to the principal's office for punishment and finding that after you face up to your crime, you are not disciplined but rather wrapped in love and understanding beyond your comprehension. He put all the hospital staff on alert, effectively removing any chance I might have had to enact my plan. Kit betrayed my trust and braved my anger to save my life.

It was Dan who said he could literally see God's light surrounding me constantly, that I was radiating it. I found this unlikely and told him so, but he was undeterred. Dan was a deeply mystical man, and he faithfully followed the spiritual traditions of his tribe. Whatever it was that he saw in or around me beckoned to him. Dan said, "God is with you." He said this over and over, and he would not stop asking, "Tell me about your God, Roxanne."

One day we sat on a bench in a sterile, white hallway where Dan told me what he believed about the Great Spirit and the Circle of Life, and in return, I explained to him some of what Christians believe. I told Dan that I no longer believed in God myself, or if there was a God that he had abandoned me long ago. Dan looked right into my eyes and told me that I was lying—he said it was impossible that I could not believe in the Being who so obviously held me, infusing my body with light and life in spite of my subjective perception of darkness and death.

Initially, when I went to group sessions, I would not speak. Unknown to me at the time, my silence had led my fellow patients to speculate on just what could have been so terrible that I could not even give it voice. When finally, after countless group sessions, I spoke my deepest, most shameful secret—I was a pastor, and I had fallen in love with someone who had been part of my church—they all leaned forward, waiting for more.

Someone asked, "Then what happened?" I said, "Nothing. I ended it." People looked at me with confusion, saying, "That's it? You fell in love? But, was someone murdered? Was a crime committed? All you did was have an affair, and you think you deserve to die because of it? All you are guilty of, girl, is being human."

It was completely anti-climactic to them. They actually seemed disappointed that my confession was so mundane, not even scandalous by their assessment, and to my utter amazement, they all continued to act in friendship towards me. This group of intimate strangers looked at what I deemed to be the blackest part of my soul, and they did a sort of communal shrug.

They did not brand me "liar" or "adulterer." They called me "human." They called me "sister." In a non-religious setting, with people who were not all Christ-followers, I got to experience church at its best. They lived out grace towards me.

❧ 4 ❧

Unmoored

Every relationship we have ties us to life. By the time I was admitted to Brookhaven, I had severed so many relationships that precious little was keeping me on this side of the grave. One of my strongest remaining ties was also my most unhealthy—my relationship with Tony. Though I loved him deeply, ours was a toxic combination. I could not seem to break free from him physically, mentally, emotionally or spiritually.

During my first weekend at Brookhaven, I found a fiction book in the hospital reading room. It told the story of a corrupt cop who was made to pay for his vicious actions in a terrible and gruesome drama. In the book, several criminals broke out of prison and, one by one, they tortured and executed all those he held dear. They started with his colleagues and continued by brutally murdering his wife, kids and entire extended family. He was made to suffer unspeakably, powerless to protect his own, until finally he also was killed.

As I read this book, I got the crystal clear picture that should I plan a future with Tony, my children and I could very likely become victims from the fallout of his way of life.

This was not something I was willing to do. Imagine, finally healing from your own darkness only to be destroyed because you chose to live in close proximity to someone else's. By the time I finished reading that book, I had also, in the depths of my own soul, finally and irrevocably severed our connection.

This break was terrifying. As abusive as that relationship had been for me, as many times as I had returned to the last place he and I had been together to attempt suicide on the very spot, as much pain and heartache as I had endured in loving him, even so, he had helped hold me to the planet. Our bond was strong, passionate and deep, beyond words. When I broke it, I experienced that break in every cell of my body. I felt completely unmoored.

❧ 5 ❧
Two Roads Diverged in a Wood

A few times over the course of my stay at Brookhaven, the chaplain spoke with me one on one. We were connected by the fact that we were both ordained women in ministry, but as we talked I was to learn that we had another experience in common. She, too, had suffered clinical depression at one point in her life.

As she shared with me her story, I was struck by the uncanny similarities in the path we each had walked. Yet, there was one glaring difference. Instead of abandoning her emotionally and physically in the midst of her illness, her husband had stood beside her. Though she made unhealthy relationship decisions that caused great pain to those around her, though she became a version of herself unrecognizable to all who knew her, though she would have given up and thrown away everything precious to her, he refused to leave her alone in the darkness.

Instead of checking out and finding comfort for himself in the company of a different lover, he did all he could to help. And when he did not know anything more to do, he stayed. He fought. He held on to his love for her. He took care of her and of their children. Rather than getting stuck in anger and resentment, he chose to be her champion, doggedly believing in her and in their love and in the life they had made together even when she was no longer able.

It was not easy, yet it made all the difference in the world. Her depression never went as deep as mine, and she healed much faster. When it was over, her life and her family remained intact.

Now, I confess that I do not know what hell my former husband endured during my illness. I cannot imagine how terrifying it was for him to watch me slowly disintegrate, how powerless he may have felt as I slowly spiraled further and further away from him and into insanity. He simply did not have the strength, courage or knowledge to help me. At this point in my journey, I choose to have compassion for him. I am very clear in the knowledge that depression does not only affect the person who is diagnosed. All who love that person suffer, too. It is a difficult situation, and people navigate it in a variety of ways. Most do the best they can.

At the time, however, as I listened to the chaplain speak of her husband's actions in the midst of her depression, all I could think about was how my own life might have turned out differently had I been married to a man who was capable of that kind of love and commitment. She and I walked the same road through a dense and frightening forest. When the pathway split, the strength of her husband enabled her to choose the path leading more quickly into sunlight. The path I took, on the other hand, led me more deeply into the dark.

Laughing Again - Roxanne Reneé

❧ 6 ❧

"If you can't come out, I'll come in"

When my cousin, Sandy, with whom I shared a deep bond from years past but with whom I had not spoken in a very long time, learned that I had been admitted, she sent a very personal letter to me at Brookhaven. Sandy had walked her own path through hell, and though she was not without her scars, she had emerged from that path with strength, wisdom and an authenticity that drew others to her and made them feel safe and accepted, no matter what they had done, no matter what been done to them. A former addict who worked tirelessly as an Alcoholics Anonymous sponsor helping others find their way, Sandy gave voice to lessons that guide me to this day.

Tragically, Sandy died in a motorcycle accident less than a year after writing me that letter. I choose to share excerpts from it now not only to document the way her love reached across distance and time to embrace me in my darkness and fought to pull me back toward life, but also to honor this strong, beautiful and inspiring woman.

Dear Roxanne,

I know you're in a lot of pain, and I want you to know I DO understand. I can't say I've been through the exact same things as you, but I'm willing to bet they are similar, that the "feeling" is the same.

My first thought when I learned of your struggle, your deep guilt over being divorced even though you are a pastor, was anger—anger at the church, or "organized religion" I should say. I don't mean to condemn religion in general, but I have strong feelings regarding religion as opposed to "spirituality," which is a very different thing in my book.

Religion can be good for some people when it provides structure, fellowship and support. It may be the only thing a person ever comes into contact with to "lead them," so to speak, to God. I had my time with "religion," too.

As a child who had been in Sunday school and church, I rebelled "down the wrong road" all those years with drugs and alcohol, and then I landed smack in the middle of a very charismatic movement that I must say, in all fairness, saved my life at the time.

But during the time I was with that church, I was told it would be a sin to divorce my husband. It did not matter how abusive things were. None of that seemed to matter to the church or the pastor. So, I stayed in that awful relationship for four and a half years, going crazy myself. Then, I woke up.

It dawned on me that, no matter what, God would not want me to be so unhappy. The Old Testament is just that—the old testament. The New Testament speaks of love, kindness, forgiveness, etc. God WANTS me to be happy. I had tried all I could, and it was time to move on, save myself, period.

Now in doing so, I ended up losing custody of my children. Obviously that is not what I wanted or felt I deserved,

VERY PAINFUL. I'm sure you're now knowing how that feels, and I'm so very sorry to hear of your similar plight. My heart goes out to you. I truly DO know how extremely painful that is.

I drank over that for several more years, turning my back on God because I felt HE had turned his back on ME. Eventually, through a series of events, I got my God back. Only this time it was SO different. It was not the God of organized religion. What I found was spirituality and a personal relationship, a belief that works for me. I happened to find it through Alcoholics Anonymous, and thank God I did.

Anyway, to get to my point, it is my belief that religion produces guilt and shame. Spirituality produces forgiveness and acceptance and healing. When a church preaches sin and damnation, it leaves no room for mistakes (which I prefer to call Lessons), no room for forgiveness.

In AA, I work with a lot of people who have been damaged in the name of religion, but God is about acceptance, love, forgiveness and tolerance. So if you've felt guilty and shameful about your "lessons," don't! EVERYONE in this life has problems (some are of their own making, some are not)—lessons to learn, to live through, to have pain over, to make amends for, to heal from. You are still human. God forbid you be human??? It's ok.

I have also learned in the past eleven years that I CAN survive without custody of my children. It was so painful in the beginning I thought I would die. I WANTED to die. It was so excruciatingly painful not to have them that at times I thought it might have been easier if THEY had just died. Then, I could mourn their deaths and go on.

Do you know what I mean? It was just so painful to have to deal with the horrible, never-ending custody battles—it was a War Zone for years! I'm their MOTHER...I should never have lost custody. That must mean I'm a bad mother. I knew somewhere inside myself that I was not a bad mother, but society looks at you like that anyway.

I had guilt and shame that I knew I didn't even deserve, but I carried it around anyway. I took it willingly, and unwillingly. It appeared that I did not have a choice then. I wore that guilt and shame until the weight of it broke my back. Sure, I'd done some things that were not perfect, but did I really deserve this? It took me four long years to come out of my own shock and begin to work on some sort of healing from my loss. I pray you don't wait that long.

There is something I learned when I got to AA, some-thing that saved me: Everything happens for a reason, and I don't always get to know why. I apply that to everything. It helps.

I remember when I first lost custody there were people who would say, "Oh Sandy, you'll see the good in this one day." I wanted to CHOKE them. I thought, how could anyone be so cruel to say such a thing?

Truth is, I have seen good come of it. I call them "God-inci-dences." I run into people everywhere who need to hear my story. They need to hear that they are not alone, not the only ones, and I've discovered that talking about my situ-ation helps me, too. For the longest time, I could not talk about it. The shame kept me silent. Now, I will talk about it to anyone, anywhere, and it's healing both ways.

I still don't know "why" this happened to me. I still think

(in my humanness) that it was "unfair" and that I did not deserve it. But, I also trust that I don't know The Plan, that I'm not the only one on a Path.

For some reason, known only to God, my children were put on a path of some pain of their own. No, it's not "fair," but perhaps they have to experience those things so that later in life they will be able to help another. I don't know. And, I don't need to know. I just need to trust God, trust that as long as I do what is in front of me today, His Will will be done in my life. I may not have all I want, but I certainly have all I need. And more, if truth be told, you know?

So most of all, I guess, I want you to know that I DO understand about losing children. I ABSOLUTELY know what that feels like, no matter what the particulars are. It's a pain only a mother can know; I believe that.

I also believe that this pain will NOT kill you. You ARE strong enough to make it through. We are strong people. I know what it feels like to want to just wither away and die. Because it's too hard. Too big. Too painful. But it's not; it's really not.

There IS light at the end of that tunnel. Walk towards it. I know you can do it. Please don't waste years of your life like I did. CHOOSE to stand up. Forgive yourself now. You deserve forgiveness. It's already done.

I was going through some old things recently and found some reminders of my loss. I sat there remembering how I isolated so much in those days. No one knew what to say to me, and I didn't really know how to behave either. Do I have the right to laugh and be happy? How dare I? That kind of talk to myself—very defeating—you DO have the right to be happy.

Here is something else I use often. When something is really bothering me, a problem that hasn't been solved yet, I deal with it for a certain amount of time on this particular day. When I've done what I can on this day and cannot do anymore, I put it on a "shelf" inside of me, and I go on about my day, having a good day. If it rears its ugly head again that day, I literally picture a stop sign in my head, say to myself, "Stop! I will not think/dwell/fret on this again today. I will wait until tomorrow." And I force (train) myself to think of something else.

Another thing I've discovered over the years is that when I go to bed at night and I say, "Thank you, God, for a good day" (I say it even if on that particular day some-thing seemingly awful happened), I discover that I mean it. That no matter what—I'm alive; I'm relatively healthy (if I take care of myself); I have friends and family who care; I'm clean and sober; I have food and shelter; my limbs work; I can see and hear...the list goes on.

Gratitude is an AMAZING thing. I believe it can truly turn us around. I really do. And when I've said, "Thank you, God, for a good day" a whole bunch of times, guess what? LIFE IS GOOD. No matter what my losses. No matter what my pain. It's ok. Life can STILL be good. I deserve that, and so do you.

Godspeed, Roxanne. I'm praying for you.

Love,
Sandy

7
Arrogance and Choice

Though I experienced countless interactions, individual sessions and group sessions with the therapists at Brookhaven, two encounters stand out in my mind. The first was with the director of the hospital, a former pastor and gifted counselor. I was brought to his office to speak with him after he learned of my plan to complete suicide at his hospital.

He asked me questions in order to understand what was driving me so powerfully toward a self-inflicted death. In addition to my belief that death would stop the ceaseless physical, mental, relational and emotional agony of my clinical depression (a belief for which I had no proof, but to which I clung with zealous desperation nonetheless), I was suffering due to my spiritual beliefs.

I had come to believe that I was a source of evil in the lives of those I loved, most importantly, in the lives of my beloved children. I felt like I brought them only darkness, that my inability to get out of a relationship with a violent man placed them in danger and that if I were dead they would be safe. Further, having always had a strong sense of morality and justice, I had become judge and jury in my own life, and I had decided that my sins were so horrible that I deserved to be punished—I deserved to die for my self-labeled crimes.

The director listened for a while, and then he said, "So...that thing Jesus did on the cross, that wasn't good enough for you?" Startled, I sat there and looked silently back at him. He continued, "That thing God did on the cross, involving Jesus and forgiveness for all sin for all time, that wasn't good enough for you? You think that your sins are so bad that only your death can atone for them, that somehow your sacrifice has more power than what God did?"

I was stunned. With one question, he masterfully peeled away my powerful desire for self-punishment to reveal my own deep-seated arrogance. I had survived quite a bit in my life, and I had developed a belief about my own strength and my own ability to succeed. On some level I had lived my life believing that because I did the right things, because I was "a good girl," because I was a hard worker, I had earned the strength to rise above previous difficult life circumstances. I had never really needed forgiveness, never really needed grace, because I had never really failed before now.

On some level, I believed that because I had been such a good girl, I did not deserve to be sick. Why hadn't God healed me when I had served God so faithfully for my entire life? Deep down, I was really angry about what I perceived to be a lack of justice. God wasn't being just, so it was up to me. I stepped into the role of Judge.

And now, now that I had fallen so far and done such wrong in my own eyes, now that I was completely unable to save myself, now that I really needed grace, I had decided that I did not deserve to get it for free. Arrogantly, I had taken the place of God and decreed that I, and I alone, must atone for my crimes. No one else's sacrifice would suffice. Killing myself was an act of penance in my mind, but it was penance that no one required, no one...but me.

The second encounter with a therapist at Brookhaven that stands out in my mind occurred during a group session. We were discussing triggers and other things that could cause us to relapse back into depression after we had healed. I found this discussion curious because it assumed that we would indeed heal, and I was not convinced of this at all.

In spite of my skepticism, I was following the discussion, and when it came my turn to participate, I did. When asked what circumstance could drive me back into suicidal depression in the future, I answered, "If anything ever happened to one of my kids...if I lost one of them... I would again become suicidal."

The therapist said, "That's not true." I was enraged.

How dare she tell me how I would or would not feel were one of my children to die! I'm sure my expression communicated my horrified and angry disagreement with her statement, so she continued, "If that were true, Roxanne, then every parent who has lost a child would enter a suicidal depression, and that simply does not happen."

I was speechless in the face of her logic. She was right. Every parent who loses a child does not commit suicide. As I absorbed this fact, I realized the truth: should the most horrific thing I could imagine ever happen, even then I would not necessarily have to relapse. I had a choice. I would always have a choice.

❧ 8 ❧

Surprise Appearance

One morning, we were meeting for one of the ceaseless group therapy sessions. The therapist had us singing Christmas carols. We went around the room, person by person, and stated our favorite carol. Then, the group would sing the carol together.

It was probably meant to be uplifting, but I experienced it as grating. Imagine, trying to sing songs like "Jingle Bells" and "Deck the Halls" when your soul is filled with so much pain that the simple act of breathing is almost unbearable. Like nails scraping down a chalkboard, it made my nerves feel even more raw and exposed. I ground my teeth together and suffered through it, singing very little.

When it was my turn to choose the song, I picked "Let All Mortal Flesh Keep Silence," not your average, everyday Christmas carol. This haunting hymn in a minor key had long been one of my seasonal favorites, but no one else knew it. So, they asked me to sing it aloud for the group.

I closed my eyes and began to sing. A hush fell over the room as the notes rang out, pure and clear. I actually got lost in the music. Time seemed to stand still. I had not lifted my voice in song for years, and I'd truly forgotten what it sounded like, what it felt like.

When I finished, I opened my eyes and looked around the room. People were weeping. Somehow, the thing that happened when I used to lead people in worship via song and prayer, the way that the Spirit used to show up and connect with people through my words and my music in a way that completely transcended my own self, that thing mysteriously and miraculously happened again—in spite of my depression and in spite of my inability to subjectively "feel" the Spirit's presence at all.

I noted their reactions as a scientist watching something from a distance, feeling detached and somewhat bemused. How and why did Spirit choose to make that kind of appearance in the midst of a contrived and cliché Christmas activity during group therapy at a mental hospital? It was interesting, but it didn't feel particularly connected to me. Little did I know at the time that God's interaction with me was about to become downright insolent.

❧ 9 ❧

Surrender

It was evening. I trudged into the cafeteria-turned-makeshift-chapel for the Christmas Eve service and took my seat in a hard, gray, metal folding chair. Outside, it was sleeting. Inside, the cheap holiday decorations seemed garishly out-of-sync with the dark emotions and pain of those present.

There we gathered, a hodge-podge of patients suffering from mental illness, chemical dependency, eating disorders, and neurological trauma. In my row sat the wretched of the earth—a young man who kept banging his head and muttering unintelligible words, a paraplegic, a woman whose body had wasted away to 80 pounds and a man who easily weighed over 400, a drug addict, an alcoholic fresh from prison, two men with bipolar disorder, a schizophrenic woman with post-traumatic stress disorder and me—suffering from this depression so deep that I had been admitted to a hospital, for the fourth time that year, to keep me from taking my own life.

For days, the Holy Spirit had hounded me relentlessly. This was strange, as I had not been on speaking terms with God for some time. The Spirit said to me: *I want you to thank me for the gift of this depression.*

My response was cold rage. The gift of this depression? In the midst of this depression, I had lost everything: my marriage, family relationships, my home, my church, too many friends to count, my health, my personality, my children, my mind, my faith, my song, my very self. I had no place of my own to live, no job, no family nearby and no means by which to pull myself out of this nightmare that had become my life.

In the three years since the birth of my twins, no traditional or alternative medicines, no type or amount of counseling, no hospitalization, no prayers had brought me healing. Multiple doctors had recommended electroshock therapy for my "treatment-resistant depression." I had lost hope that I would ever be well.

I want you to thank me for the gift of this depression. Over and over, all day long, *I want you to thank me for the gift of this depression.* I hate this depression. I hate myself. I hate you. *I want you to thank me for the gift of this depression.* No fucking way.

The worship service was excruciating. Locked inside a mental institution, with my little boys, my friends and my family far away, I wondered how my life could so completely disintegrate. I wondered how the boundary that separates having-it-all from having-lost-it-all could be so frail, so thin, how we can walk so close to it for so long without any idea of the danger. I could not feel God's presence at all, not even in that irritating demand for gratitude.

After the service, I prayed on my knees with my face on the cold, hard cafeteria floor, begging God for healing. The chaplain and several others prayed with me. Nothing happened, nothing. I felt foolish and completely, utterly forsaken.

Hours later I went to bed, and again came the command: *I want you to thank me for the gift of this depression.* I was weary beyond description as I thought back over years of fighting—first to live, then to die. I had no strength left to fight.

And I got it: I could be in the darkness without God, or I could be in the darkness with God. Either way, I was still in the darkness, with no guarantee of healing, but the only Source of Life that I know is God.

"Fine, God, I surrender. Thank you for the gift of this depression," I said, without conviction and with more than a little attitude.

Again, Roxanne. Are you kidding me? Unbelievable.

Say it again. "Thank you for the gift of this depression." I repeated it over and over until, with still no sense of healing, my sleeping pills took affect, and I fell into a dreamless slumber.

Laughing Again - Roxanne Reneé

❧ 10 ❧

Snapshot

It had been an awful day, waiting for the interminable hours to pass and trying to forget that it was Christmas. All day long, I doggedly and oft times sullenly repeated my mantra of obedience: Thank you for the gift of this depression. I said it hundreds of times.

Not only was God harassing me, Cali kept asking me to pray and sing with her. I find it ironic that you can be locked in a mental institution, deeply dysfunctional and actively suicidal, yet when people find out that you have been a pastor, they still think you somehow have a direct line to God. Irritably and really just to shut her up, I had finally agreed, and we were sitting together on a hospital bed at 9 p.m.

I don't remember much of what we prayed. I do remember that at some point we began to sing a praise chorus, and as our voices blended in harmony, I felt the heaviness of depression lift from my being, literally felt the physical sensation of painfully unbearable weight lift from my chest. This feeling lasted only a few moments, then it crashed back down with force, but that was long enough to give me physical proof that my body was capable of healing.

It was like having a snapshot of what could be possible in the future. I felt like God's message to me was—regardless of your belief that you are no longer capable of healing, Roxanne, you are.

No matter how real or deep the darkness, no matter what the facts of my experience had been to date, my belief that I had passed a point of no return was a deception. When I said my mantra later that night, it was with slightly less bitterness.

❧ 11 ❧
A Drug Cocktail

The day after Christmas, I was in the psychiatrist's office for a medication check. The doctor was flipping through my chart, noting years of failed treatments.

"Nothing has worked on your depression thus far. At this point, anything we do is a guess. We are going to try an experimental medicine combination, a drug 'cocktail' if you will. We just learned about this, at a conference two weeks ago, to help with treatment-resistant depression. We are going to try small dose of Effexor™ and a small dose of Remeron™, both antidepressants. In addition, we are going to give you a small dose of Depakote™ and a small dose of Seroquel™. Though you are not bipolar, and you are not psychotic, these additional meds will enhance the effectiveness of the two antidepressants. In addition, we will have you take Restoril™ for sleep."

"Sure," I thought, "why not? Thank you for the gift of this depression." But aloud, I said nothing.

"And we will be discharging you in two days. Your insurance coverage has run out."

The words echoed in my head like a death sentence.

I'm going back to Kansas City to die, I thought. Panic made it hard for me to breathe.

Then the calm, clear words spoke into my being yet again: *I want you to thank me for the gift of this depression.* So, in sheer obedience, I did.

"Thank you for the gift of this depression," I breathed out, and I got up and went to see the nurse who would dispense my new med cocktail.

❧ 12 ❧

Dawn, Reborn

I was sitting in a booth in Montana Mike's Steak House in Miami, Oklahoma on December 28, 2000 with three other people. Conversation was awkward. What do you say to someone who was just released from a mental institution not because she is no longer suicidal, no longer anxious, no longer depressed, but because she has reached her insurance coverage limit for the year?

They were discussing their plan to keep me safe from myself until January first, a new insurance period, when I could be readmitted to the hospital. Their plan included rope, to tie me to a chair if need be, and 24-hour surveillance. I was thinking about how to call the number I had in my pocket of a drug dealer back in KC, in order to get what I needed to finally kill myself.

Then, quietly and without warning, everything changed. I felt a monumental spinning, shifting of energy within my body, like something that was upside-down or backwards righted itself. I cannot describe this mysterious phenomenon except to say that I felt like I, who I am fundamentally, the Roxanne who I had always been before the depression but who I was convinced was dead and gone forever, that "me," somehow returned and took up residence once again in my body. I looked at the clock. It was 7:15 p.m. My depression was gone.

What happened? Was it my surrender and my subsequent offering of gratitude in obedience, even though I could not feel it, an act of my spirit? Was it the new medicine combination taking effect in my body, a physiological phenomenon? Was it some mysterious combination of the two? Experts may argue, but I believe it was the act of my spirit in response to God that set the stage for everything physical that came afterwards.

Now don't get me wrong. When my depression lifted, I was not instantly well. I still had a lot of hard, healing work ahead of me, for I had much to grieve and much to rebuild. I would have to end unhealthy relationships, and with gritty determination, I would have to fill the empty space my depression left with life-affirming thoughts, life-affirming actions and new, life-affirming relationships. I still had to heal from the Panic and Anxiety Disorder and Post-Traumatic Stress Disorder, get a job, find a place of my own to live and regain primary care of my children.

Yet, on that winter night, my spirit was resurrected. I experienced and thus became my name—Roxanne Reneé means "dawn reborn." This literally was the rebirth of daytime for me; after a long darkness, I got a second chance at living.

PART II: Dawn, Reborn

As I share my story with you now, I claim both the praise and the promise of the words written in the ancient letter to the church at Ephesus, words that can be found in the New Testament of the Christian scriptures. I claim the praise and the promise for myself and for all of us who seek to be well—

> Now to God, who is able to do immeasurably more than all we ask or even imagine according to God's power that is at work within us, to God be the glory forever and ever.
>
> Ephesians 3:20-21

This is not the end of my story; it's really the beginning. After my experience at Brookhaven, I was told not to get "too excited" about being healed because I had a 90% chance of relapse, would be on meds indefinitely and would likely be in and out of the hospital for the rest of my life. How depressing is that? I always thought my psychiatrist should have served up that news with a shot of bourbon.

Regardless of what he said, I decided not to accept this information as the only possibility for my life. My personality is a bit rebellious and I tend to question authority. In this case, that's a good thing. Through significant scientific research and ongoing practice, I developed an intentional lifestyle that has kept me depression-free to this day and off meds since January 2005. I share it with you in the next section.

PART III

7 Secrets to Live Well Today

❧ 1 ❧
There's Something You Can Do

Before I understood the impact that lifestyle has on mental health, I thought depression was something that just "happened" to me, like I was happily living my life one day and the next thing I knew I was stuck in the throes of a deadly illness so debilitating that I could not even use the power of my own mind to help myself heal. This view of the illness leads to a sense of powerlessness and despair, something those who suffer from depression know very well.

I lived with an underlying terror that though I was healed, at any moment the darkness could descend upon me and take over my life once again. It was the psychiatrist who told me not to get too excited about being healed who also gave me the clue I needed to begin researching. He said, "Do not, under any circumstances, for the rest of your life, ever, ever, ever allow yourself to become sleep-deprived again."

"What?" I thought to myself. "You mean there is something preventative I can do to avoid relapse?" Indeed, there is. In fact, there are seven lifestyle practices I have found that keep me mentally well, and I have been utilizing them for years.

While I am living proof that these lifestyle choices work, I don't want you to simply take my word for it. Do your own research; there is a lot of data available. I recommend starting with the excellent book, <u>The Depression Cure: The 6-Step Program to Beat Depression without Drugs</u> by Stephen Ilardi, PhD. I read about Dr. Ilardi's work in a December 2007 issue of <u>Newsweek</u>, and I was excited to learn that *the same lifestyle choices I had found to prevent my own relapse actually heal clinical depression!*

Dr. Ilardi's groundbreaking book describes a clinically proven program to heal from depression and stay healed, and he gives us an in-depth look at six of the seven lifestyle practices that I utilize and teach. Though his book does not address my seventh practice, the practice of spirituality, he would not deny its impact on mental wellness. Most important for practical purposes, Ilardi's book outlines a 12-week plan for implementing what he calls Therapeutic Lifestyle Change. It is an invaluable resource for all those who want to heal from depression, avoid relapse or simply better support their own long-term mental health.

So, what are these lifestyle choices? I call them "The Secrets of Mental Mojo" or "The 7 Rs—7 Daily Lifestyle Practices to Support Mental Wellness." The 7 Rs are Restore, Refuel, Reset, Rejuvenate, Relate, Refocus and Renew. The first five Rs are physical lifestyle practices that affect our internal mood. The last two Rs are internal wellness practices: how we manage our mind and how we manage our spirit. I've stacked the 7 Rs, one on top the next, from those that are most basic (restore, refuel, reset) to those that take more effort (rejuvenate, relate) to those that require the most determination and vigilance (refocus and renew).

Laughing Again - Roxanne Reneé

❦ 2 ❦

RESTORE —
the impact of sleep

Every day, we need to restore our bodies with adequate rest. Sleep is so foundational to our health that we die faster without it than without food. During sleep, our bodies repair, process all kinds of data, and store information in memory so that we can be prepared for the next day.

Our brains simply cannot work well without good sleep. When we do not get adequate sleep over time, a whole host of problems develop: we get sick more easily due to immune system dysfunction; we increase our risk for heart disease; we experience impaired brain function that includes a decreased ability to regulate glucose, cortisol and insulin (thereby increasing our risk of obesity and type 2 diabetes); we suffer reduced brain efficiency in terms of memory, learning, creativity and problem-solving; we experience an increase in accidents and errors; and we have an increased incidence of depression and anxiety.

If you find that you experience nightly sleeplessness for three weeks or more, you have insomnia and need to do something to correct it. Many who suffer from depression also have a sleep-related breathing disorder, such as sleep apnea, which contributes to their insomnia. According to research cited by neurologists, people with persistent insomnia are 40 times more likely to develop depression within a year than those who sleep well. When we go without any sleep for three or more days in a row, we can actually become psychotic. In the first section of this book, I shared that I went over eight months without a solid night's sleep. It's really no surprise at all that I developed clinical depression.

In order to be well, we need to get seven to nine hours of sleep *every night*. You will know that you are getting enough sleep when you consistently awaken before your alarm goes off, feeling rested and refreshed. Going to sleep is really a habit, and there are several things we can do to cultivate good sleep.

One thing we can do is go to bed and get up at the same time each day. Another thing we can do is to invest in a quality mattress. Think about it—if we spend one third of our life there, shouldn't our bed be comfortable? In addition, it's important to follow the same routine each night when preparing for sleep and to make sure that pre-bedtime activities are relaxing. Avoid caffeine and alcohol in the evening, as they disturb normal sleep patterns, and reduce or quit tobacco use, as it can also interfere with sleep. When hungry before bed, try a light protein snack, preferably something with tryptophan like turkey or tuna or milk; it helps to induce sleep. Do not exercise immediately before bed; that can wind you up.

Further, set up your bedroom as a place for sleep and sexual or relaxing activities only—no computer, no television and no workout equipment. All these things send your brain the message to wake up and get moving. If you cannot remove these items from your bedroom, at least consider covering them or placing a screen between them and your bed.

If you find yourself lying awake in bed, unable to fall asleep for more than 15-20 minutes, get up. Divert yourself to another activity until you feel sleepy. Make a list of any thoughts in your mind; sometimes getting them down on paper is all it takes for your brain to relax and allow you to sleep.

Finally, about an hour and a half before bed, turn off the computer and bright overhead lights, and turn down the thermostat. When light fades and temperatures drop, our brains get the signal that it's time to wind down and prepare for sleep. If you practice good sleep habits, you will find over time that you naturally fall asleep and sleep well.

If you are practicing all these habits consistently and still have trouble sleeping, check with a medical professional. There may be another cause for your insomnia. The sooner you find a way to restore your body with consistent, good sleep, the sooner your brain will function well.

Laughing Again - Roxanne Reneé

❧ 3 ❧

REFUEL —
the impact of nutrition

Every day, we need to refuel our bodies with good nutrition. While there are many aspects of nutrition that are important for overall health, I focus upon four that have a dramatic effect on our brains: sugar, omega-3 essential fatty acids, water and vitamin D.

Processed sugars

Neuroscientists have recently shown us that sugar is powerfully addictive, able to light up the brain's pleasure centers just like cocaine or heroine. This discovery came as no surprise to me—processed sugar has been my mood-altering drug of choice for years.

Some people self-medicate with alcohol or drugs, but for me it's brownie batter. I mixed brownie batter and kept it on hand in my fridge. When I felt stressed about something, I'd shove three or four big spoonfuls of brownie batter down my throat, and within minutes I would literally feel the calm flowing down my body in waves. I was the "poster child" for pressure eating. It wasn't always brownie batter, anything chocolate with high sugar content would work—Swiss Cake Rolls™,

Cosmic Brownies™, Zingers™, candy bars, cake, ice cream. I'd experience a brief period of perfect calm, followed shortly thereafter by a nosedive in both my mood and my energy.

Processed sugars dramatically affect mood, and due to their inflammatory effect in the body they are a major player in depressive illness. It was my personal trainer, Julie, who taught me the value of limiting my processed sugar intake. In order to help me lose weight, she had me eat a diet of lean protein, complex carbohydrates, fruits, veggies, low-fat dairy and healthy fats while limiting my processed sugar to less than 20 grams per day.

At first, as you can imagine, I had what I can only describe as withdrawal symptoms. I had been easily eating 100 grams of sugar every day, many days more than that. I was not alone in my sugar overload. Americans eat processed sugar in almost all our foods, and we drink it avidly. Soda, for example, has an average of 69 grams of sugar per 20-ounce bottle. That's over 17 teaspoons of sugar in one drink! As an average, the typical American consumes some 25 teaspoons of sugar each day, totaling an astounding 80 pounds of processed sugars each year.

After the initial days of discomfort as I weaned off processed sugar and learned a new way to eat, I discovered an interesting thing: not only was I losing weight, my moods were more even. I did not have the dramatic ups and downs to which I had been accustomed.

Turns out, the feel-good neurotransmitter serotonin is made out of an amino acid called tryptophan, and tryptophan is abundant in foods like turkey, chicken, fish, beef and pork, as well as in beans, milk, eggs, soy and cheese. In my new diet, I was gaining the benefit of ingesting less inflammatory sugar while simultaneously increasing the raw materials my body needed to produce serotonin. No wonder my moods evened out and my energy stayed consistently high!

To support your own mental wellness, I recommend making it your goal to consume less than 30 grams of processed sugar each day and to make sure you are eating a consistent supply of foods rich in tryptophan. When counting your daily grams of sugar, you do not need to count the natural sugars found in fruits and vegetables, for these are not hazardous to your brain in the same way processed sugars are.

Further, I recommend that you avoid neurotoxic artificial sweeteners. Instead you can use, in moderation, natural sweeteners like honey (which is anti-inflammatory and has other health benefits), stevia (also called sweet-leaf), and xylitol. I actually carry stevia packets of natural sweetener with me everywhere I go.

I still enjoy eating sweets, but it's rare for me to use them as mood-altering substances. I've learned to handle my stress in better ways. So nowadays when I want something sweet, I fulfill my desire by eating fresh fruits, by using natural sweeteners and by eating processed sweets only in moderation. In our home, anything with more than 10 grams of sugar per serving is considered a dessert, so it's a treat we really savor rather than everyday fare.

Omega-3

You've likely been hearing a lot about omega-3 in recent years, and you may even be currently taking a supplement of fish oil that is high in omega-3 fatty acids. But what are omega-3 fatty acids? Technically, they are polyunsaturated fats, fats that are liquid at room temperature and that remain liquid when refrigerated or frozen.

These "good fats" are profoundly important for our health because each and every cell in our bodies is surrounded by a cell membrane composed mainly of fats. This membrane allows proper amounts of nutrients to enter the cell. It also ensures that waste products are efficiently removed. For a cell to work properly, to hold water and vital nutrients, to protect us from damage by toxins and to be able to communicate with other cells effectively, the cell membrane has to be healthy and fluid.

Because cell membranes are composed largely of fats, the quality of our cell membranes is directly related to the quality and amount of good fats that we eat. When we eat lots of saturated fats that are solid at room temperature, this results in cell membranes that are hard, lacking fluidity. When we eat a diet rich in unsaturated fats that are liquid at room temperature, we produce cell membranes with a high degree of fluidity, and this is promotes wellness in every organ and every organ system of our bodies.

For our brains specifically, fats count. Every neuron in our brains is constructed of these crucial building blocks. In fact, the human brain is composed mostly of fats. While we can internally manufacture most of the fats our bodies need, we cannot make the fats known as "essential" fatty acids. We must eat them in our food. Omega-3 is one of the two essential fatty acids; the other one is omega-6.

Omega-3 is found in green things (leaves of plants, algae and grasses), and in things that eat green things— like fish and grass-fed beef, for example. Omega-6 is found in nuts and grains and in things that eat grains—like most of our livestock. We get omega-3 when we eat things like flaxseeds, hemp seeds, some dark green leafy vegetables, certain types of algae, wild game and cold-water fish such as salmon, tuna, halibut and herring. We get omega-6 when we eat things like grains, corn oil, safflower oil, sunflower oil, canola oil, processed foods, fast foods, grain-fed beef, grain-fed chicken, bottom-dwelling fish, shrimp and crab.

Nutrition experts teach that our blood should have, at most, a ratio of omega-6s to omega-3s in the amount of

2:1, and a ratio of 1:1 is ideal. However, the average American eating the standard American diet has a blood ratio of omega-6 to omega-3 that is wildly out of proportion. Research documents the American diet at a shocking 16:1 up to 26:1 ratio of omega-6s to omega-3s.

This imbalance has critical consequences for a wide variety of conditions, especially for our brains, which cannot work as they are designed to work unless these fats are in balance. We can correct this imbalance by eating markedly less grain, or we can add significantly more green.

I encourage people to talk with their health care providers and to consider taking a minimum of 1500 mg of omega-3 every day for brain health. Personally, I take twice that amount each day. I have learned in partnership with my doctor that this dose works best for me. You may find that a different dose works best for your health.

When taking omega-3 fatty acids for brain health, it is best if you can take two forms of omega-3, EPA (eicosapentaenoic acid) and DHA (docosahexaenoic acid). Check with your healthcare professional regarding the best ratio for you of these two types of omega-3. For healing depression, some recommend a ratio of three EPA to two DHA, and others recommend a ratio of two EPA to one DHA. Other medical conditions respond to other ratios.

Read the back label of your supplement to determine the amounts of EPA and DHA in each serving. Then, if you seek 1500 mg of omega-3 each day in a 3:2 ratio, for example, you would want 900 mg of EPA and 600 mg of DHA. If you seek 1500 mg of omega-3 each day in a 2:1 ratio, you would want 1000 mg of EPA and 500 mg of DHA.

CAUTION: Some conditions need careful monitoring when adding omega-3 to the diet. Persons who have medical disorders involving bleeding, who bruise very easily or who are taking blood thinners, as well as people taking prescription blood pressure medications and/or prescription anticoagulants absolutely must consult with a medical professional before taking supplemental omega-3 fatty acids!

In order for omega-3s to function optimally in your body, its important to make sure your diet includes a sufficient amount of vitamin B6, vitamin B3, vitamin C, magnesium and zinc. Certain amino acids also aid in the absorption, utilization and function of omega-3 fatty acids, so it is a good idea to discuss your diet with a nutrition professional when and if you have questions or any kind of concern.

As supplements, omega-3 fatty acids are available as soft gels or as bottled liquids. When you purchase omega-3 supplements, it's very important to remember that these oils are highly sensitive to damage from heat, light and oxygen. Choose a high-quality, certified organic product that has been refrigerated and is packaged in a dark brown or green glass jar if it is a liquid. Be sure you immediately store the product in your refrigerator or freezer after purchase. Also, be sure you look at the list of ingredients to make sure there is no filler oil, especially not soybean oil.

Make sure your supplement is tested (or "assayed") by a third party to ensure that it's free from toxins and heavy metals and that the ingredients inside the bottle or soft gel are the same as the label claims. The label should also say that the oil is "molecularly distilled." Finally, make sure your omega-3 supplement contains vitamin E, which is a powerful antioxidant that is added to the oil to prevent the fatty acids from becoming rancid.

Your supplement should never taste "fishy" or smell bad when you take it. When it does, it's rancid, and you should not consume it. If you find you have a problem burping up a fishy taste hours after taking an omega-3 supplement, consider taking your supplement at night. If you are taking soft gels, you can store them in the freezer and take them at night before you go to sleep. I find that the higher quality fish oils have few if any unpleasant, "fishy-tasting burp" side effects.

Water

Water is essential for life. It is involved every day in myriad critical bodily processes. Our brains themselves are over 75% water, and water is directly involved in the effective manufacture of all neurotransmitters, including serotonin.

Because water is so important, dehydration affects every system in our bodies, including our brain and nervous system. When we are dehydrated, our brains cannot function well. By the time we "feel" thirsty, we are already dehydrated.

I recommend drinking 1/2 the number of your body weight in ounces of unflavored water each day. If you weigh 160 pounds, for example, your goal would be 80 ounces of water each day. It is important to drink plain water because sugars and flavored substances stick to each water molecule. Plain water can pass more easily into our cells and is quickly available for use. When you drink other fluids, especially dehydrating ones like coffee or alcohol, make sure you drink extra water, over and above your daily goal, to replenish yourself.

If you have trouble finding ways to drink your daily amount of water, try the following routine. Immediately upon rising in the morning, drink a full 12-ounce glass of water. Then, subtract that amount from your total needed and divide by two. So, in the above example, 80 ounces minus 12 ounces is 68 ounces, and 68 ounces divided by two is 34 ounces. Fill a cup with 34 ounces of water and make it your goal to drink that amount by noon. Then refill your cup with 34 ounces, and make it your goal to drink that amount by dinner. After dinner, stop drinking so that you are not up all night running to the bathroom! It helps me to use a water bottle with a straw; it just seems an easier way to drink.

CAUTION: If you have a medical condition in which water accumulates in the body and is not processed normally, such as congestive heart failure or kidney disease or any condition involving excessive release of anti-diuretic hormone, do not adjust your water intake without first consulting your doctor!

Vitamin D

Vitamin D is actually a hormone that is responsible for unlocking hundreds of genes in our bodies, thereby controlling the daily function of our nerves, blood vessels, brain, heart, bones and skin. Most people suffering from depression have very low blood levels of this vital nutrient. Vitamin D is important in fighting depression not only because it regulates gene function in the brain and other body systems in ways that support wellness, but also because it is potently anti-inflammatory (and chronic inflammation contributes to depression in a variety of ways).

Even though our bodies are able to make vitamin D when the sun's ultraviolet rays penetrate our skin, most of us living in industrialized nations do not get the vitamin D we need. The practice of fortifying dairy products with vitamin D has not helped, either, because the D2 used in milk is not the same as the D3 made in our bodies.

How can you know if you are getting enough vitamin D? Go to your doctor and request a simple blood test to determine your vitamin D level. If your vitamin D is low, you can take an inexpensive supplement based upon your doctor's prescription. Or, you can get more bright light on a daily basis, and I will discuss this in the following chapter.

❧ 4 ❧

RESET —
the impact of sunlight

Our bodies were designed to be outdoors, and for most of human history that is exactly where we spent most of our time. For the past 100 years, though, those of us living in America and in other industrialized nations have been spending more and more time inside. While indoor lighting provides around 100 lux (lux is a measure of the intensity of light), the natural light on an overcast day is 1,000 lux, and the natural light on a sunny day ranges from 10,000 lux to 100,000 lux!

Natural light is important for our health in several ways. When the sun's ultraviolet rays penetrate our skin, they begin a process that converts cholesterol into vitamin D. This natural production of vitamin D will give us what we need, provided we get the right amount of exposure. The amount of exposure needed varies based upon the time of day, the time of year, the place you live, the weather and your own complexion. Experts suggest that, wearing a swimsuit, the amount of time in the sun you need to synthesize that day's vitamin D is equal to the amount of time in the sun you need to develop a very faint hint of a tan. Sunscreen dramatically decreases the amount of vitamin D our skin can produce, so if you are out in the sun to get a kick of vitamin D, put on sunscreen after you get enough exposure to make your daily dose.

How much time is needed to make vitamin D? In the continental United States, between 11am and 3pm, from May to August, if you are not wearing sunscreen, 10-15 minutes a day should do it. In September, October, March and April, you need to double that amount of time. If you are dark-skinned, it will take longer. Unless you live in a sunny place like Florida or Arizona, you may want to consider taking a vitamin D supplement from November through February, based upon your healthcare provider's recommendation.

Another way that natural sunlight impacts our health is through our eyes. We have special receptors in our eyes that connect straight into our brains, and these receptors only respond to the brightness of sunlight. When these receptors don't get the light they need, and most of us don't, there are major effects for our body clock and for our brain chemistry.

Our brains keep our bodies running smoothly by means of a cluster of neurons known as the "body clock." This body clock stays accurate as long as it gets enough bright light each day. When it does not get enough light to reset itself each day, our hormones get out of balance, we have trouble sleeping and our energy levels rise and fall at inappropriate times. For those of us who are sensitive, these changes can trigger an episode of depression.

Bright light not only resets our body clock, it stimulates the brain to produce serotonin. This important neurotransmitter boosts feelings of wellbeing, propels us to seek social contact, makes us less likely to fight with others and calms our brain's stress response. Bright light, thus, has an antidepressant effect, and it tends to do so much more quickly than drugs like Prozac, which can take several weeks to begin working.

How much sunlight exposure do your eyes need to reset your body clock and produce serotonin? It varies, but most of us need only 15 to 30 minutes each morning (wearing no sunglasses) within two hours of rising. It is very important to remember that the timing of bright light exposure for mental wellness is important and individualized.

For detailed instructions on the amount of bright light that may be right for you, I recommend that you read <u>The Depression Cure</u> by Stephen Ilardi, PhD. If you still have questions or concerns, consult with a doctor or healthcare professional who understands the use of bright light therapy.

If you cannot get outside where the light is at least 10,000 lux on a daily basis for 15 to 30 minutes, consider a light box. It's a convenient and reliable way to get a daily dose of bright light that will reset your body clock and stimulate your brain to produce serotonin. The most widely researched type of light box for treatment of depression is one that uses fluorescent bulbs to provide 10,000 lux of white (broad-spectrum) light. Personally, I use the Caribbean Sun Box because it is small, lightweight and portable for travel.

When using a light box, follow the manufacturer's instructions regarding the positioning distance from your head. It's best if you set it in front of you and 6 inches above your eye level, so it hits your eyes at the angle of the sun. If you have to set it to one side, switch it to the other side halfway through your exposure period. Don't stare straight at it (which will cause eye strain); rather, focus upon something in front of you.

CAUTION: Some conditions, especially eye problems, are made worse when using a light box. Diabetics with eye complications can be adversely affected. Also, persons with bipolar disorder or seizure disorder should never start bright light therapy except under their doctor's supervision. It's always a good idea to check with your doctor before starting any new treatment.

❧ 5 ❧
REJUVENATE —
the impact of
breathing and movement

Breathing

I learned how to breathe from Julie, the personal trainer I mentioned earlier who also taught me how to eat. Not literally, of course—I'd been breathing my entire life, and as a vocalist I knew how to breathe strongly and deeply. Rather, Julie taught me how to breathe in ways that calm and center me, ways that pull me from frenzied activity or frantic thought into quiet focus, ways that allow me to navigate my anxiety and even my panic with success.

Julie taught me how to breathe when she taught me the practice of yoga. Before I began to practice it, I thought yoga was something solely for freakishly limber people who could contort themselves into myriad shapes just to make the rest of us look stiff. I am not limber to this day, and I had never imagined myself in a yoga class. Then, my struggle with anxiety manifested physically in the form of dangerously high blood pressure. I did not want to immediately take medication, so I made a deal with my doctor to remove some of the stresses in my life and to take a restorative yoga class.

What I did not know at the time is that physiologically yoga affects the vagus nerve, helping to balance our autonomic nervous system. This is our largely unconscious nervous system, classically divided into our sympathetic and parasympathetic nervous systems. (I will discuss these two systems in the section on movement). In addition to affecting the vagus nerve, yoga poses stretch and wring out our muscles and organs. This delivers oxygen to our cells, removes toxins and releases stored molecules of emotion (neuropeptides) which at times can result in a rush of previously unprocessed feelings.

Thus, I cried my way through my first three yoga classes. It's not that the poses were uncomfortable—they really were, but not enough to make me cry. No, I was releasing "stuck" emotions that had been contributing to my anxiety and my high blood pressure. If that were not enough, I felt awkward and off balance and inflexible and out of place. I felt frustrated and angry and sad and irritable. I felt challenged and confused and overwhelmed and tight. I felt all these things in every part of my body, and as I felt them I was continually reminded to focus on my breathing.

The practice of yoga is a practice of breathing through the uncomfortable positions in which we find ourselves.

After you practice yoga for awhile, you start to notice that out in the real world when you are feeling awkward or off balance or inflexible or out of place, when you are feeling frustrated or angry or sad or irritable, when you are feeling challenged or confused or overwhelmed or tight, you keep breathing. And this is like a miracle—for getting oxygen to our brains and to all our cells is profoundly calming, energizing and healing. It allows us to focus, to think clearly and to process information in helpful ways. It allows the brain to work the way it was designed to work. It dramatically reduces anxiety and the damaging stress response.

Think about how your breathing changes when you feel excited, about a time you gasped in surprise or delight. Think about a beautiful experience that literally took your breath away. Now, think about a time you felt afraid, about your heart pounding in your chest. Recall your gasp of horror or outrage. Think about an awful experience that made you actually hold your chest so tightly that you stopped your breath. Good or bad, happy or sad, our emotions are intimately connected to our breath. Every feeling we have about every experience of our life affects our breathing. The reverse is also true; the way we breathe affects the processing of our emotions and has the power to shape each experience of our life.

Without breath, there is no life. This is why humans have always connected the breath to the life force, the spirit or soul. Across all times and cultures and geographies and spiritual belief systems, focused breathing has been used as a tool to move the mind into a state of deep calm.

I invite you to try it for yourself. Begin by simply paying attention to your breathing patterns. Note when you are taking regular breaths, when you are taking deep breaths and when you are taking shallow breaths. Note how your body feels in these different states. Note how your feelings change when you consciously change the way you are breathing.

When you are feeling anxious, take five to ten minutes and practice a few yoga poses while focusing upon your breathing. If you have never practiced yoga, you can enroll in a class or follow a DVD to begin learning. I recommend the YoGo™ workout DVD warm up for five minutes of easy, calming yoga (see References and Resources).

Another thing you can try when you are feeling anxious is deep, even breathing: breathe in for a slow 6-count and then out for a slow 6-count. Place your hand on your tummy and make sure you breathe deeply enough that your abdomen expands as you inhale. Feel the air move into all areas of your lungs; feel your ribs expand. As you exhale, draw your stomach muscles back towards your spine. Push the air out from all areas of your lungs; feel your ribs move back together. Five to ten minutes of this deep breathing is usually all I need to significantly decrease my anxiety and clear my mind. Some days, though, I need another kind of breathing altogether.

CAUTION: This next method of breathing, a variation of a technique called "Breath of Fire," is not for everyone. Do not practice it during menstruation or if you are pregnant. Practice it with caution if you have high blood pressure, heart disease, epilepsy, vertigo, acid or heat related gastric problems like ulcers or if you have suffered a stroke. Stop if you get dizzy. As always, if you have any concerns or questions, it is best to check with a medical professional for guidance.

On days when I am frustrated or angry or anxious, needing to "blow off steam," and am unable to engage in physical activity for some reason, I practice a variation of Breath of Fire. Breath of Fire itself is a yoga breathing technique that clears your mind and sometimes your nose as well, so it's a good idea to keep some facial tissue handy! Breath of Fire oxygenates your blood, which provides energy to your cells and facilitates the elimination of waste and toxins. It massages your internal organs, promoting digestion. It builds lung capacity and strengthens your respiratory system. Most important to me, it helps to balance the nervous system.

Sit up in a comfortable position. Elongate your spine upwards, and align your spine with the back of your head by bringing your chin back and in, like a soldier at attention. Rest your hands comfortably on your thighs, and close your eyes. While the original Breath of Fire utilizes shallow inhales and exhales (almost like panting), this variation begins with a deep inhale through your nose. Then, push hard with your diaphragm and stomach muscles as you exhale through your nose with short bursts.

When initially practicing this technique, do it for one minute. Inhale deeply through your nose, then push your breath out through your nose in 7 short bursts as described above. Repeat for 60 seconds. As you master the technique, you can slowly increase the amount of time that you practice this kind of breathing. Be careful not to hyperventilate, and if you ever feel dizzy or lightheaded, return to slow, deep, even breathing until you feel normal again.

Movement

For years, we have heard myriad reports about the benefits of exercise for our health. There are so many voices recommending so many options that it gets a little overwhelming, and people who suffer from depression already feel overwhelmed. So let me reassure you: the amount of exercise needed to stop depression and to change your mood is less than you may think.

Exercise is a medicine that works on the brain in ways more powerful than any drug. Exercise increases the activity of brain chemicals like serotonin and dopamine more effectively than antidepressant medications like

Zoloft. Exercise stimulates the production of a key hormone (brain-derived neurotrophic factor, or BDNF) that repairs the brain damage caused by depression. Exercise sharpens concentration and memory. Exercise helps us focus and think clearly.

Regular exercise stops the body's stress response in its tracks. In a stress response, our sympathetic (fight-or-flight) nervous system is engaged: we experience shortness of breath, a rush of adrenaline, increased blood pressure, increased heart rate, decreased circulation and decreased "feel good" brain chemicals. This is important if we are, say, getting ready to fight or flee from a tiger.

Our bodies were designed to remain in the fight-or-flight state for about an hour. After an hour, you are either safe from the tiger, or you are in the tiger—threat averted. Our bodies are then supposed to return to their relaxed state and stay there until faced with another life-or-death situation.

Unfortunately, in modern life we continually engage our fight-or-flight stress response, to both real and imagined threats (our bodies don't distinguish between the two), and we tend to stay stressed, never returning to our relaxed, natural state. This never-ending stress response contributes significantly to depression.

After experiencing a stressful situation, we need to engage our body's parasympathetic (rest-and-digest) nervous system response that slows and deepens breathing, decreases blood pressure, decreases heart rate, increases circulation, and increases "feel good" brain chemicals like serotonin and dopamine. Movement is the best way to get there, and it has no harmful side effects like so many of our medications. As we move our muscles, we burn sugar, increase respiration and increase circulation. This makes plenty of oxygen available for combustion and metabolism to give us energy, so we don't need to rely on a kick of adrenaline or a cup of coffee.

The next time you're feeling stressed, take a good hard walk, and see whether you still feel as stressed afterwards. Or, if you don't have time for a long walk, simply move in a different way for two solid minutes. Try running up and down stairs, balancing on one leg, alternating jumping jacks with sit-ups, practicing yoga poses or dancing with abandon to some music you love. Even a few minutes of movement can alter your mood.

I experience this transformation first-hand all the time. Something will happen that leads me to feel stressed, anxious, angry or down. In earlier years, I would have grabbed something chocolate and stuffed it in my mouth, but now I put on my walking shoes, call my best friend on my cell phone and head outside. Let me be clear—when I head out on my walk, I am still feeling all my negative feelings. I am not happy about taking a walk. I am not serenely enamored with the truth of any of the wellness lifestyle practices I teach. I force myself to take a walk anyway.

Then, I spend the first half of my walk engaged in a process I call "venting," by which I mean I verbally express all my displeasure. It's not pretty—it's a kind of verbal and emotional vomiting—but I do it while I'm using my muscles to walk, hard, to the point of being slightly out of breath. My best friend, who knows how this works, wisely listens without judging me or trying to fix me. Without fail, I begin to feel less awful. And every time, even after years of doing this and even though I forced myself to do it with the knowledge that it physiologically will change my brain, I am a bit surprised that I start feeling better. My negative energy has been worked out, verbally and physically, and by the time I reach the halfway point my mood unfailingly shifts. (You should know that on some days the halfway point is farther away than on others!)

Movement also works if you don't have time to take a walk. Some days, I actually wake up in such a bad mood that I find myself groaning over the idea of having to hang out with my own self for the rest of the day. At that point, I turn on music from the 80s (or some other uplifting-to-me playlist), and I get up and dance around my house. I don't feel like it, but I force myself to sing the lyrics and to keep dancing. It's hard to stay in a dark mood when you are singing and dancing to fun music. I usually end up laughing at myself before I'm done, and that is a much better way to start the day.

For your exercise to have a long-term antidepressant effect, you need to engage in 30 minutes of aerobic activity three times a week. This amount of aerobic exercise, in the form of a brisk walk, has been clinically proven to stop depression. Walking is something that we were designed to do, something that requires no special exercise equipment and something that people of all ages can do any time of day, in almost any kind of weather, with or without others. When we walk outside in the sun with a friend, we engage in three wellness lifestyle practices at once!

Remember these things about antidepressant exercise: work out for a minimum of 90 minutes each week, evenly spread over the course of several days; make it aerobic, by which I mean it needs to raise your pulse to a rate some-where between 75% and 90% of your maximum heart rate; warm up for five minutes beforehand to reach your target heart rate; take the time to stretch out afterwards so you avoid muscle soreness; choose activities that you enjoy and that you are capable of doing with some measure of success; make it part of your schedule so that it becomes a habit to exercise at the same time on the same day several times each week; devote an hour to your exercise routine (this gives you time to change clothes, warm up, work out and cool down); make it engaging, purposeful and/or fun (enjoy the beauty outdoors, listen to music, walk the dog, work in the yard, walk to get somewhere or walk while talking with a friend); and enlist someone to hold you accountable.

Initiating activity

People in the throes of depression have a hard time getting up and starting anything new. This is because a part of the brain, the left frontal cortex, does not function properly when people are depressed, and the left frontal cortex is the area of the brain that initiates activity. When I was suffering from depression, I remember knowing that I needed to exercise. I would sit on the couch and think, "I really need to exercise. I know exercise will help me feel better. I used to exercise a lot. I just don't feel like getting up off this couch. Why can't I just force myself to get outside and walk? I really need to exercise. I know a walk will help me feel better. I never used to have a problem getting myself to move! God, I'm such a loser. I don't even have the strength or discipline to get up and walk. I suck. I'm so weak. I hate myself. I'm such a lazy slug. I'm never going to get better." And on it went—I would add a self-loathing rant to my inertia, all the while never moving from the couch. But, if a friend came over, I was somehow able to get up and get out and walk with my friend. This was a mysterious phenomenon to me at the time, but with the knowledge I have now, it makes perfect sense.

Here is the truth: in people who are depressed, a part of the brain is broken, but not beyond repair. If you are currently depressed, please stop berating yourself! Remind yourself that you can and will heal. Until then, be kind, gentle and patient with yourself. Enlist a friend or several friends to serve as your temporary left frontal cortex. These people can help you by initiating fun activities and times of good connection and by keeping you accountable to your wellness practices.

And if you love someone who is battling depression, volunteer to serve as that person's temporary left frontal cortex. Be the one who initiates contact. Be the one who plans uplifting activities. Be the one who makes sure your depressed friend gets out and gets involved. Help your loved one stay on track as he or she implements healthy lifestyle choices. According to clinical research, it only takes three months of practicing the 7 Rs for a depressed person to experience improvement, and your friendship can provide essential and practical healing support that makes all the difference in the world. In fact, social connection is so healthy for us that it stands firmly as one of the critical lifestyle practices for ongoing wellness.

⚜ 6 ⚜

RELATE —
the impact of social connections

The Good

Several years ago, I was dealing with a difficult situation regarding my children and their father. I was talking one day with a girlfriend, who was also going through a particularly difficult time regarding one of her children and his father. I asked her, "Why are we each going through this alone?" and we hatched the idea for a weekly prayer group for moms. The original intent was that we would pray for our children and for one another and provide support for parenting.

This group of eight moms has been meeting in my home every Wednesday morning for five years now, and though we still pray and talk about our kids and motherhood, the focus has expanded so that our prayer and our conversation encompass the whole of our lives. This is sacred time for us; we literally schedule our lives around it. These relationships ground our lives. We eat together. We laugh together. We cry together. We keep the faith for one another. We ask each other the hard questions. We celebrate large and small victories together. We keep each other accountable. We give each other grace.

When one of us is doubt-filled, we hold up the mirror of friendship and help her to see the best of herself, the way we see her. When one of us is afraid or grieving, we go into the darkness with her so that she need not be there alone. When one of us needs practical help with kids or a home project or a job lead or relationship issues or the recipe for a certain green smoothie or a great vacation deal or a work-out partner or even bail money, we step up and make it happen. This group is a refuge, a safe harbor in which to rest when life's seas are stormy, and I know that I can count on them to love me both because of myself and in spite of myself, as I also love each of them. Together, we continue to navigate life crises that easily could have sucked one or more of us into despair and clinical depression.

I realize each day how profoundly blessed I am to be a part of such an amazing group of women, to be able to call them my friends. Though it is hard-wired deep into us to connect with others, essential, in fact, for our wellbeing, many people in modern society lack this kind of profound, life-giving connection. Research reveals that one quarter of all Americans report no intimate social relationships, and one half of us report having only one close friendship. Research further reveals that disruption of social support increases the risk of depression, while having good social support is strongly correlated with healing from depression.

It is extremely unfortunate that one of the characteristics of depression is withdrawal; this insidious disease pulls us away from that which can help us heal. Even when we are not depressed, we tend to live such busy, isolated lives, relentlessly pursuing achievement, money, career advancement, social status and material possessions, always thinking we will make time for our friendships and family relationships another day. Yet if we are not intentional about nurturing our relationships, that day never comes. And none of those things we pursue has the power to protect and heal us the way social connection does.

When we are deprived of contact with other human beings for even a few days, there are physiological consequences. Certain biological processes become unbalanced; stress hormone levels rapidly rise while energy and mood rapidly fall. Conversely, when we are in the immediate vicinity of others, even pets, our body's rhythms will synchronize, and we will feel calmer.

This innate need to be in connection with others is a legacy from the time when humans lived as hunter-gatherers. In those days, being alone meant certain death. Though it is possible in our modern world to physically live alone (eat alone, sleep alone, reside alone, work alone and play alone), we have not been able to escape our brain's psychological need for connection with others. Considering the fact that psychological or emotional events initiate, and are in turn influenced by, chemical and electrical processes within the body, it's not surprising that they effect our physical health.

There is an intriguing 20-year study by Harvard medical doctor and sociologist Nicholas Christakis and political scientist James Fowler that reveals how emotions can pass among a network of people up to three degrees of separation away. That's right: happiness is contagious and can actually be passed to you from your friend's friend's friend, someone entirely unknown to you! Google "Christakis and Fowler" to read more about the social contagion of behaviors; it's fascinating, and it gives us a whole new paradigm for how people get sick and how they can stay healthy.

Another very interesting finding, this one by Alan Deutschman, an author and consultant who studies what makes people change, is that people change not through sheer force of will or even threat of impending death but rather through an emotional relationship with someone who inspires belief and hope, someone who has successfully navigated the needed change. This is why mentoring, life coaching from someone who has "been there" and support groups like Alcoholics Anonymous can be so profoundly helpful in getting us unstuck. Deutschman's book, <u>Change or Die</u>, unpacks the how-to and the why of it all and would be good reading if you want further information on this topic.

A third piece of research that I want to highlight is the landmark UCLA study of women friendships. This study suggests that women respond to stress with the release of oxytocin, a hormone that buffers the fight-or-flight response and encourages them to gather with other women and tend the children. When they engage in the "tending and befriending" behaviors, more oxytocin is released, calming them and further countering stress. According to this research, women's brains have a built-in way to counter stress. Why is it, then, that women are currently twice as likely as men to experience clinical depression? I think the answer is multifaceted, but we certainly contribute to the problem in the way we push our friendships to the back burner when we get busy with work, family and life in general.

Study after study shows us that having social ties reduces risk of disease, lowers heart rate, lowers cholesterol, lowers blood pressure, keeps us living longer and keeps us living better. Researchers conclude that not having social connections is as dangerous for your health as obesity or smoking. For men and for women, we can no longer operate under the belief that friendship is something to only do "one of these days when things settle down."

It is absolutely imperative for wellness to regularly spend time with people who breathe life into you! You know these people—when you are with them, you have no sense of time. When you leave them, you are full of good energy and eager to see them again. With them, you laugh. With them, you feel safe. With them, whatever your soul needs for nurture, it gets. Studies show that treatments for depression that improve our interpersonal relationships can be as effective as medication, and more so, over the long haul.

From this point forward, I want you to look at time spent cultivating your relationships as one of the most important investments you can make in your own health, in living well. I strongly encourage you to give yourself regular doses of good social connection, daily if possible. Though face time is absolutely the best social interaction for wellness, phone calls and video calls are also ways to connect. Email, instant messaging and texting are not as helpful, as it is difficult to transmit and decode emotion via these media. Start now to schedule time with life-givers, and keep your commitments with the same discipline you would employ in taking a life-saving medication.

The Bad

What if the social relationships in which you find yourself do not breathe life into you? What if, no matter what

improvements you try to make, you have one or more relationships in your life that are toxic? If you can, end the
toxic relationship. I've been where you are, and I had to
make that decision myself. I understand that this is a
wrenching, sometimes even dangerous, decision. However,
your brain will never heal from depression while being
subjected to ongoing verbal, spiritual, emotional and/or
physical abuse and the unrelenting stress response that
abuse creates. If you need help reaching a safe place, call
the National Domestic Violence Hotline at 1-800-799-SAFE
(7233) or TTY 1-800-787-3224.

What about toxic relationships that are not abusive
as above? Or, what about toxic relationships you cannot
easily leave, those with a boss or family member, for example? I advise you to find ways to limit your time with these
toxic people. Instead, spend extra time engaged in healthy
and nurturing relationships and activities. Learn how to
create healthy boundaries, and build up your own mental,
spiritual, emotional and physical strength.

When I must spend time with someone who sucks the
life out of me (an "energy vampire," if you will), I make sure
there is a set start and end time. I plan the encounter, if I
can, on a day that I am feeling strong and good. I avoid
upsetting topics, and I direct the conversation or activity
toward something fun or at least something emotionally
neutral. Finally, I make sure I schedule a nurturing activ-

ity or time with a life-giving friend both before and after the encounter. This practice allows me to maintain any necessary contact with toxic people while suffering little if any side effects from our interaction.

And the Ugly

Depression turns us inward where we tend to focus on our own ugly drama, but when we turn our focus outside ourselves and get involved in helping to heal some of the ugliness in the world, paradoxically, we actually feel more happiness. This is not just an esoteric teaching; it is backed up by hard scientific data.

Dr. Richard J. Davidson, Neuroscientist, Professor of Psychology and Director of the Laboratory for Affective Neuroscience at the University of Wisconsin-Madison, has spent many years studying the brain structures behind depression, anxiety and addiction as well as happiness, resilience and compassion. His studies on Buddhist monks reveal that when they are specifically engaged in compassionate practice, their brains show both increased activity in the prefrontal cortex (flooding them with a sense of wellbeing) and increased activity in the areas of the brain involved with motor planning (preparing their bodies to jump into action and help relieve suffering). That's right, the practice of compassionate service not only helps us to feel better ourselves, it empowers us to do something that makes the world better, too.

In <u>The Power of Intention</u>, author and teacher Dr. Wayne Dyer cites an intriguing study. In this study, those who received a random act of kindness experienced a statistically significant increase in immune system parameters, including an increase in serotonin levels. Those who performed the random act of kindness received the same boosts, and so did those who only *witnessed* the random act of kindness! The National Institute of Health in Maryland released a study showing that committing unselfish acts stimulates the brain's pleasure center, and according to a study conducted by the Ontario Ministry of Health in Canada, those of us who volunteer tend to have less heart disease, lower incidence of premature death and fewer overall health problems. Serving others improves our self-esteem, enhances our immune system, reduces our blood pressure and decreases our stress response.

I think it's brilliant that our brains are designed in such a way that when we invest ourselves in something good, some act of love or kindness or compassion, everyone benefits. Even on days that the best you can muster is a simple prayer for someone else who is hurting, that act of service and compassion draws you out of yourself and your own pain. In order to add a communal aspect to your healing acts of service, consider getting involved in a church, support group or volunteer organization. I encourage you to make it part of your wellness commitment to regularly help others in some way. You'll be happy you did.

❧ 7 ❧

REFOCUS —
the impact of thoughts

Feelings and thoughts

Though I am capable of logical and intense thought, my emotions always seemed the major force in my internal world. They colored my mind every day, and this affected every interaction in my outer world. One could argue that this is a rather adventurous way to live, not knowing when you awaken how you are going to feel and therefore not knowing how your day is going to unfold, but it's certainly not a way of living powerfully or well. My shifting emotions seemed mysterious to me, a side effect of my hormones or an unconscious response to some event, always beyond my control. I often said, "You can't control how you feel; you can only control how you choose to act." Turns out that's not exactly true.

It occurs for most of us that first we do something, then we get something, then we feel happy. For example, I work really hard to finish an extra project at work; I get a bonus, and then I feel great about my job, my finances and myself. What happens, though, when I work really hard to finish that extra project at work, and I don't get a bonus or any recognition at all? Then, I feel resentful, think resentful thoughts and act in resentful ways, which causes others to react to me negatively, which ends with me not feeling great about myself or my job and can ultimately threaten my finances.

What if we changed it around? What if we chose to be peaceful and content and let our actions flow from that place of contentment? We would still work hard to finish that extra project. Whether we got a bonus or not, people would respond to us in positive ways. We would feel good personally, and we would feel good about our job, creating an attractive emotional climate that would enhance productivity and effectiveness. It seems to me that those people who, in spite of circumstances, create positive energy in our world ultimately experience personal rewards, social rewards and often times financial rewards as well.

Though many of us live our entire lives completely unaware of the profound way our thoughts and our words shape our feelings, the truth is that they do. For example, I can choose that I am going to be grateful. I can choose grateful thoughts even when I do not feel grateful. At this point, it really is an exercise in discipline. I can say, "Thank you for the gift of [you fill in the blank]" just as I did during the time I was hospitalized at Brookhaven for suicidal depression, a time that I most certainly did not feel grateful. When it is simply too difficult to name anything in the present, painful situation a "gift," I have learned that simply saying "thank you" every time my mind seeks to chew over the ugliness of the situation, then immediately getting engaged in something different, is also very helpful. (In the next section, I'll go into more detail about why and how saying "thank you" supports our mental wellness).

Without fail, what we "focus on" expands. As we practice over and over thinking grateful thoughts and saying grateful words, we begin to notice things for which to be grateful. Finally, we begin to actually feel grateful. As I've applied this practice again and again in my own life, and as I've seen it applied again and again in the lives of others, I have been forced to accept the fact that in many cases you actually can control how you feel. The way you feel grows out of the way you think and the words and actions that flow from your thoughts, and in most cases thoughts are things you can choose.

What I'm talking about, of course, is cognitive behavioral therapy; it's really helpful in a variety of situations and invaluable as a lifestyle wellness practice. What happens, though, when you are stuck with a negative or anxious thought repeating over and over in your head (resulting in a negative or anxious feeling), and you cannot seem to stop it? I call this "being in your hamster head" (think about what hamsters do running on their wheels:

they run the same ground over and over, never getting anywhere). The technical term for this kind of thinking is "rumination." Rumination is, not accidentally, the same word for the digestive process of cows (chewing things over and over and over with the goal that they will eventually become digestible). Unfortunately, rumination or "being in your hamster head" does not eventually help you stomach the issue at hand; it just keeps you stuck in a dark and very unpleasant place in your head while your body remains stuck in the physiological cascade of chemicals and reactions we know as the stress response.

Earlier I said that without fail, what we "focus on" expands. This is true for both positive and negative thoughts. When we ruminate, our dark thoughts and feelings get bigger and bigger. We do less outer-focused activity, and we withdraw from others. The more time we spend alone and idle, the more we tend to ruminate. It's a vicious cycle.

How to stop ruminating

Breaking the cycle of rumination involves first becoming aware when you are doing it. When I catch myself beginning to have thoughts that are negative or anxious, I stop and talk back to my thoughts. I literally hold up my hand in the stop gesture and say, "Not helpful."

I do not recall who first taught me this brilliant response to my panic-filled brain, but I've been using it for years. If I argue with myself, trying to reason myself out of my dark imagery and mind chatter, I prolong the rumination. If I try to pretend that I'm not really feeling bad or if I chastise myself that I "should" not feel this way, I feel worse. If I say, "Not helpful," I give my brain the message, without judgment, that I currently need to focus on something that is helpful and that I am open to revisiting these thoughts at another time should they ever become helpful. This response, saying "Not helpful," gives my brain the cue that, next, I am going to engage in something that indeed is helpful. Immediately, my stress level drops a notch.

It can also help me when ruminating to remind myself that thinking is a function, not a reality. I've learned to observe my thoughts and not take them too seriously. When I notice myself getting really hooked by some situation or person, I try to step back to a more objective place, and I say, "Isn't that interesting? I wonder why I'm thinking that thought? Isn't this response interesting? Isn't this mood interesting?" In this way, I allow my thought or my mood to be a separate thing, to move through me and pass out of me rather than making it The Truth.

Next, I take action. If my rumination is over a situation that may need my attention at some point or if I simply need to give expression to my thoughts, I give myself a limited amount of time, five to ten minutes, to write down a to-do list or to journal my thoughts or to map out a plan on my calendar. I time it, and at the end of this time I take another action.

For me, the most consistently quick way to get out of my "hamster head" is to talk with a friend while taking a hard walk. My mind can be a dark and scary place; sometimes it's best for me not to go in there alone. In conversation with a good friend, I can give voice to my fears or sadness. I can release my anger or frustration. I can be heard. I can get help solving a problem. I can be given a fresh perspective. I can even be made to laugh. Because conversation is so engaging, as I talk with and listen to my friend I am pulled from the darkness in my head to a place of more balance, a place that's not "all about me" but rather about life beyond me.

Even if I cannot talk with a friend while I walk, the aerobic activity of the walk itself is powerful enough to shift my mood, as I discussed in the chapter entitled, "Rejuvenate." Other anti-ruminative activities include doing anything with someone else (volunteer, play a game, even cleaning your house can be fun with the right company!), listening to music or audio books or comedy, watching a compelling movie (not everyday TV, which actually leads to rumination because the programming simply is not absorbing) or practicing one of your hobbies.

If you struggle with rumination, and we all do at times, the key is to be prepared. Make a list of ten or more things you find deeply engaging and enjoyable. Keep it close at hand so that when you begin ruminating, you can quickly redirect yourself. In addition, look through your schedule each day and each week to find times you may be alone and idle. Intentionally schedule engaging activities for these times.

Guard your mind

Also, I think it's imperative to guard what you let into your mind in the first place. In terms of the stress response, our brains don't tend to subconsciously reason out, "That tornado is on TV, not by my house. That man with the machine gun is shooting at a person in Iraq, not me." Rather, they tend to see these images and react with a primal fight-or-flight response, dumping stress chemicals into our system.

Further, disturbing and violent images tend to replay over and over in our minds. Images have a much greater impact on us than when we read about or hear a report on a violent situation. I have made it my practice to avoid the television news or to limit my exposure to it. I certainly don't watch it before bed. I usually get my news from sources I can read or hear, and I am very discerning about when and how long I will give my attention to negative topics. Likewise, I avoid violent, angry or disturbing movies and books; there is enough drama and horror in the real world for me.

I'm even intentional about my music choices. If I'm in a dark or sad place, I refuse to enhance and prolong my stay there by listening to music that brings me down. It's not that I never listen to sad or angry songs; I do. I'm just thoughtful about when I choose to do so. If I've really been struggling, then you can bet I'll be playing songs that lift me up.

Singing along to a favorite tune is even more powerful for redirecting our thoughts than simply listening to music. It is not a mystery to me why I felt my depression lift for a brief time while I was singing on Christmas night in Cali's room at Brookhaven. Music is sound, a traveling wave of energy. We cannot remain unaffected when it hits us. Because music is vibration, it literally moves us on some level. When we sing along, we are physically producing vibrations; we are moving our energy around. Singing is a way to release emotion; singing is a great way to shift your mood. "Music hath charms to soothe a savage breast" so the saying goes, and it's true. The next time your thoughts turn savage, try turning on some upbeat or uplifting music and singing along.

Manage your mind

Sometimes it's not rumination over an external event that drags my mood and my energy down. Sometimes it's that voice in my head that I call my Inner Critic. Let me tell you, she is mean. Through this voice, I say things to myself that I would never even think of saying to another human being. You know this voice. It's the voice that tells you that nothing is ever good enough; in fact, it tells you that *you* are not good enough, and then it goes into great detail explaining all the ways in which you are not good enough. My therapist once told me that I needed to talk as nicely to myself as I would talk to my best friend, or at least as nicely as I talk to my dog. It's good advice. So, when my Inner Critic steps up to begin her nasty lecture, I hold up my hand in the stop gesture and say, "Not helpful." Next, I intentionally say something kind or affirming to myself. Then, I redirect myself into some engaging activity.

Let me tell you how I use affirmations to help manage my mind. "Thoughts become things," says author, entrepreneur and speaker Mike Dooley, and I have seen this principle at work. I select a goal that I want to achieve or a state of being that I want to experience. At times, I will select a Scripture or a reading that resonates with me as Truth. I write these out in first person, present tense, usually on index cards. So, for example, rather than writing, "I will lose ten pounds," I write: *I am lean and strong and healthy.* I make the affirmation present tense. Likewise, instead of writing the Christian scripture from the book of Philippians that says, "Finally, brethren, whatever is true, whatever is honorable, whatever is right, whatever is pure, whatever is lovely, whatever is of good repute, if there is any excellence and if anything worthy of praise, dwell on these things," I write: *I dwell on whatever is true. I dwell on whatever is honorable. I dwell on whatever is right. I dwell on whatever is pure, whatever is lovely, whatever is of good repute. I dwell on excellence and things that are worthy of praise.* I make the affirmation first-person, or personal, about me.

Then, I post my written affirmations in a place I will see them often (like my bathroom mirror), or I carry them with me in my purse or pocket or computer bag. I make sure I read them, aloud, frequently. This practice trains my mind, and my brain works to find ways to make my affirmations become my reality. Through this practice, I harness the power of my mind to help create the life I desire. I manage my mind on purpose, so that it serves me.

To be effective, an affirmation needs to be phrased in first-person, present tense, and it needs to be said aloud. There is something really powerful about your brain hearing your voice claim your goal as though it exists right now. I'm not a neuropsychologist, so I cannot tell you exactly how or why this works. I just know from experience that affirmations have the most impact for you when they are said aloud, regularly, about yourself, in the present.

Remember, an affirmation by its very nature is a positive statement. This practice will not work if you focus upon what you do not want—that actually makes you more likely to get what you don't want! Think about it: when you are driving and you tell yourself, "I will not hit the tree. I will not hit the tree," what are you thinking over and over? You are thinking about hitting the tree. When you tell yourself, "No chocolate, no chocolate, no chocolate," what are you thinking over and over? You are thinking about chocolate. When you tell your child, "Don't hit your brother," what picture are you creating for him in his mind? You are creating the picture of him hitting his brother. When you say, "I failed. I cannot fail again," what are you recalling? You are remembering the feeling of failure and putting it into your present and your future.

Our words are so powerful that they create images in our minds. Before anything is ever real in solid form, it is real in our imagination. Our words create our reality. Therefore, it is imperative that we use our words to shape the reality that we want, not the reality that we don't want. Negative judgment about our past, our present or our future only hampers the inspiration and power needed for learning and success.

So, when driving, you could repeat, "I am safe. I am aware. I am a good driver." When avoiding sugar-filled treats, you could say, "I nurture my body with nutritious food." When teaching your child, you could say, "Touch your brother gently." When recalling your past and how it affects your present and future, you could say, "I learned many things that did not work. I am certain to succeed." Make it your habit, whether creating an affirmation card or simply speaking day-to-day, to speak only what you desire and to frame all your encounters and experiences in a way that is empowering rather than disempowering, then watch how you transform the world within you as well as the world around you.

Create the meaning

The final tool I want to share with you to refocus your thoughts is a tool that can actually shift your entire reaction to a person or a situation. I use this tool every day, and I call it "creating an empowering meaning." When something negative or irritating happens to us, we tend to assume that the person meant to be irritating or harmful. Then, we react in anger and defensiveness, and we send ourselves into a stress response.

For example, you may have been driving on the high-way and been cut off by a speeding driver. You may have called him a name or offered him a particular rude gesture or simply growled about what a jerk that guy is. Why did he cut you off? Why is he driving like a maniac? The truth is: we don't know. Yet, we make up a meaning that causes us displeasure and stress. Why not make up a meaning that energizes and empowers you instead?

What if you made up this story: he is not a jerk or a rude driver. He is a dad who is racing to the school to pick up his sick child. He is scared and distracted by his fear. If that were true, how would you react differently? You would probably slow down to help him get past you, and you may even say a quick prayer for him and his child. Internally, rather than being filled with anger, you would be filled with good will, and your body would not be perpetuating a stress response due to your anger.

How would your life be different if you made a habit of assuming the best rather than the worst? I don't mean sticking your head in the sand and ignoring a bad or even dangerous situation. I mean in cases where you really do not know what something "means," how would your life and your stress level shift if you chose to make up a meaning that empowered you rather than disempowered you?

Here is another example of how this works: I know a woman who just went through a grueling divorce after being married to an abusive man for almost a decade. Once she moved out, he harassed and threatened her to the point of a restraining order. He spread malicious slander about her that led to her being fired from her job and caused severe damage to her career of 20 years. Against all logic and the law, even though her ex-husband earned 13 times her annual salary, the judge did not grant her maintenance. Though her ex was so uncooperative with the legal system that it took her years and cost her tens of thousands of dollars to escape him, she was granted no legal fees. Though she invested her entire inheritance in the house that he was granted to keep in the divorce and though they shared a retirement savings, she was granted no property settlement and none of their retirement. She requested one sentimental item from that decade of her life, a fort built on their property by one of her best friends for her children from a previous marriage, and the judge did not grant her even that.

While her friends, her family and even her lawyers were outraged and dismayed at the judge's ruling, she consciously made a choice to believe that a higher power was protecting her. She decided that perhaps this ruling, in which her ex felt like he got everything he wanted while making her and her children suffer, was the only way he might let go and move on. Her ex had told her on numerous occasions that if he were ever forced to give her maintenance or if he lost any of the retirement savings, he would "never forgive her" and would "make her pay." He had already threatened her life and the safety of her children. He continued to maliciously slander her and to send hate mail to anyone who hired her for a project, and she had recently learned the shocking fact that at one time in the past, this man had literally attempted to murder another woman in his anger. So, this woman did two things: she took a long, hard look at the situation and intentionally chose to assign a meaning to this judge's unjust ruling that made her feel protected, and she learned how to use a gun, which made her feel confident and prepared.

In truth, this woman has no idea why the judge ruled as he did, and she will never know. She could spend her energy feeling abused by the legal system that was supposed to protect her from her abusive husband, but she had already tried that path during the drama of the preceding years. Feeling that way made her angry and terrified, literally sick with anxiety and resentment, and had created a stress response with significant physical consequences to her health. She decided that was no way to live. So, she chose an empowering meaning in the midst of a difficult and painful situation, and she moved forward in her life, investing her time and energy in actions that made her stronger. By choosing to manage her mind in a way that supported her health, this woman took her power back. You can, too.

At Brookhaven, I learned that when happiness is more important to you than anything else, you will indeed be happy because there will be no thoughts for which you will be willing to give up your happiness. When happiness is more important to you than anything else, you will do whatever it takes to get out of your thoughts and into a way of being that supports you. You can replace the word happiness in this paragraph with "peace" or "joy," whatever word resonates with you, but you get my point—manage your thoughts, and you will powerfully support your wellness.

❦ 8 ❦

RENEW —
the impact of spirituality

Sometimes, life really hurts. I am not one of those chirpy, religious people who try to explain away the reality of suffering. I refuse to dishonor the experience of pain by pretending it's not real, or it's not devastating.

Emotionally and physically, depression hurts. Research reveals that pain and mood share the same chemical messengers in our body as well as common pathways in the limbic region (emotional center) of our brain. When you experience depression, it is never "all in your head"; it hurts everywhere. Depression intensifies pain, and pain worsens depression.

While I won't deny the reality of pain, I do know from experience that there are things we can do to prolong it, and there are things we can do to move through it. For me, that is where spirituality comes in; spiritual practice helps us navigate the painful times of life and emerge from those times with more strength, peace and wholeness.

Forgiveness

One critically important spiritual practice for your own

health is forgiveness. Negative emotions like bitterness, resentment and sustained anger keep our body's stress response in full swing as we replay hurtful events over and over in our minds. Each time we relive the event, our body responds as though it were currently happening to us, releasing that same cascade of fight-or-flight chemicals. Internally, we are in a constant state of crisis, and this affects our health on every level.

Bitterness, resentment and sustained anger keep us stuck in the past, continually stressed and unavailable to fully enjoy our life in the present. Forgiveness is the antidote to the poison of these negative emotions.

Forgiveness is not saying that what happened is okay. Forgiveness is not forgetting. Forgiveness is not reconciliation (restored relationship), for that requires the offender to repent (admit the offense, show regret or sorrow and turn away from the previous way of behavior that led to the offense), and it requires the victim to desire a continued relationship. Forgiveness is simply this: letting go of my desire to hurt you back.

Forgiveness is a process, and the deeper the hurt is, the longer forgiveness can take. It is important to first let yourself feel the legitimate emotions arising from your experience. Emotions are chemical and electrical, and they need to flow through the body and outward for release. Talking with a trusted friend, counselor or coach, crying, journaling, yelling (not at someone, but rather as a way of expelling energy) and, especially, engaging in physical activity can be very helpful in processing your initial response to a hurtful situation or encounter.

When I am hurt, frightened or angry, I find significant comfort as I read the Psalms, the songbook of ancient Israel. The next time you are feeling betrayed by friends, read Psalm 55, or the next time you need protection from the wicked, read Psalms 140-144. This prayer poetry expresses every possible human emotion, even the dark ones, in the context of faith that *God is with us in our darkness, understands our pain and works for us and alongside us to make things right.*

It also helps me to listen to intense music with lyrics that help me process my anger or grief. What I'm describing is not pretty reading, not eloquent prayer, not tender or beautiful music; it's raw. God is perfectly capable of handling extreme emotions, so let 'em out. As I read, pray and sing, oftentimes while taking a long, hard walk, I release my emotions, and I eventually move to a place of forgiveness. It may take minutes, days, weeks or longer; I may move in then out then back in to forgiveness again, but eventually I am willing to let go of my pain.

Once you have allowed yourself space and time to process your emotions, it's time to forgive. I cannot tell you how long it will take, as it varies depending on the situation, but a good clue that it's time to forgive is when you feel begin to feel "stuck" or when those who know you well and understand the depth of your pain begin to suggest it may be time to let go and move on.

How do you forgive someone? Remember, this is you letting go of your desire to return evil for evil, to gain your own revenge, to hurt back. You forgive someone by deciding to do so and by saying, "I forgive you." If you cannot or should not speak personally, each time you think of the person or the situation, you can say, "I choose to forgive" or "I release my desire to hurt you back."

What about God's forgiveness? It's been said that though God holds us accountable for the hurt we cause, God does not hold us hostage. We may suffer the natural consequences of our actions. We may need to work to restore what we have broken. We certainly need to repent from ways of living that cause harm to others. Yet God's forgiveness, based in the love and mercy of God, is always freely available to us.

It can be hard for us to receive the forgiveness of God and others, though, when we cannot forgive ourselves. In my experience, forgiving yourself can be the most difficult of all. That judge dwelling in my own soul is harsher and more filled with condemnation than any external source, and my self-flagellation keeps me stuck in the darkness with my stress response fully activated.

I've learned over time that while this internal long-suffering may seem holy, it's not. It doesn't earn you extra time in heaven; it keeps you stuck in hell on earth. If you have committed a wrong, repent (admit your offense to God and to the one you hurt, with regret and sorrow, then turn away from your previous behavior), accept forgiveness from God and others, forgive yourself, and move on. Every time you begin to beat yourself up again for an old offense, hold up your hand in the stop gesture, say, "Not helpful," say, "I am forgiven" then redirect yourself to some other engaging train of thought or some other engrossing activity.

We cannot fully enjoy life and have energy for the present while part of us is stuck in the past due to bitterness, resentment or sustained anger. We cannot live well and happy lives if we keep our bodies in a constant fight-or-flight stress response by dwelling on negative emotions and experiences. We must choose to forgive, not for the benefit of the one who hurt us, but for our own benefit. The initial time you are hurt, it is the other who wounds you, but every time you relive your hurt, you re-wounded by your own self. Refusing to forgive is like feeding yourself poison, then waiting for your enemy to die and remaining confused when he doesn't. Free yourself from the prison of bitterness, resentment and anger; pull your spirit back into the present—choose to forgive.

Gratitude

In the previous section, I said I would explain how and why gratitude is such a powerful wellness practice. Gratitude is the antidote to worry. When we worry or when we are anxious, we are thinking about all the bad things that could possibly happen. As we imagine the worst, over and over, we kick our body into a fight-or-flight nervous system response. Remember, our brains do not respond differently to a real threat than they do to a vividly imagined threat; we get the same load of stress chemicals dumped into our system either way. With a real, physical threat, we can use this reaction to survive, but with an ongoing, imagined threat we do not tend to work out our excessive energy in a positive way. Rather, it shows up in psychosomatic illness such as chronic low back pain, chronic headache, high blood pressure, weakened immune system and a variety of other ailments.

I come from a long line of chronic worriers. Regardless of the topic, you could spend ten minutes in conversation with my maternal grandmother (by which I mean listen to my grandmother complain) and walk away so covered in negative energy that you literally wanted a shower to wash off the psycho-slime. If you weren't feeling down at the start of the conversation, you certainly felt that way by the end. Don't get me wrong; I loved this woman. I'm just clear that she was a very anxious, bitter, sad person.

The women in my family, especially, are capable of almost ceaseless rumination, what-if-ing themselves into a perpetual state of near panic. We are literally brilliant catastrophizers—we have high IQs, and we have a greater than normal tendency towards high anxiety. Put the two together, and you get to imagine, in vivid and gory detail, the worst possible thing that could ever happen in any given situation. (This is another reason I don't see terrifying movies; the movies that play in my head have provided more than enough terror for me over the years). I say, "We don't really get heart disease or cancer in my family, we just get insane." Medically translated, we get anxiety-based mood disorders and related physical illnesses such as high blood pressure. We check out or stroke out, and it's not a pretty legacy.

I have dealt with anxiety for as long as I can remember, much longer than the three to four years I wrestled with clinical depression. My anxiety fed my depression, and after my depression lifted it still took years of work for me to get a handle on my anxiety. In fact, though I have not experienced symptoms of depression for almost a decade and though I cannot remember my last panic attack, I still face and feel my anxiety every day.

I practice all the lifestyle choices I teach, and I find that gratitude is the discipline that pulls me back into the present when my worry-filled mind has gotten stuck in some bleak, frightening, stress-inducing, future scenario that has a 90% chance of never, ever happening anyway, no matter how much I worry about it. Gratitude is the antidote to worry because it grounds me in the good that I experience right here, right now. I find it impossible to simultaneously feel terror about the future while feeling deeply grateful for the blessings I have this day.

Practicing gratitude is our access to contentment and to joy. It is a powerful wellness choice because these emotions bring us inner peace and thus have calming, healing physiological effects for our body. By contentment, I mean ease of mind, satisfaction with the enough-ness of the present moment, being able to celebrate who I am right now and what I have right now. By joy, I mean the deep and abiding conviction that, no matter what the circumstance, I am surrounded and sustained by the goodness, the strength and the nearness of God who loves me beyond my comprehension and who will never, ever abandon me. Happiness comes and goes, depending upon circumstances, but joy remains even when my heart is broken and my way is unclear. Joy is grounded in faith that God with me, and God is for me.

Practicing gratitude is the path that leads away from worry and towards contentment and joy. Begin each morning, before you even arise from bed, by saying "thank you." List a minimum of three things for which you are grateful. End each day, just before you go to sleep, in the same way. You will find that there are almost always more than three things you can list. You can perform this discipline even if you are not particularly religious; you can simply direct your words out into the universe, share them with a loved one, or write them in a journal. You don't have to say, "Thank you." You can say, "I am grateful for [you fill in the blank]." The important thing for your wellness is to dwell in gratitude as often and as long as possible every single day.

Love

Another important wellness discipline is to practice love. I don't mean the touchy-feely, romantic kind of love portrayed in the movies and in popular music. I'm talking about the state of wanting and choosing the best for another. As a minister, I am asked all the time to help people discern what action is most loving in a particular situation. The simplest way I know to live from love is to continually practice kindness. You can be kind to someone even when you are angry; you can be kind to someone even when you do not like him or her. You can be kind even in the midst of a legal battle. When you practice kindness, which is a practical way to show love, you free yourself from the burdens of guilt and regret. These negative emotions can suck up your time and energy, stir up your stress response and keep you imprisoned in the past for years. Make it your habit to live in such a way that you rarely experience guilt or regret; be kind.

Further, you can show love, that state of wanting and choosing the best for another, by offering acceptance without judgment. I'm not encouraging you to accept or condone hurtful, unjust or evil actions; it is important for wellness to hold healthy boundaries and to allow natural consequences in the majority of cases. Rather, I am encouraging you to accept people as they are and to practice kindness. It is a very stressful job trying to decide universally who is good, who is bad, what the reward "should" be and what the punishment "should" be (ask any judge). It's better for your health to meet people where they are, as they are, and to be a force for goodness and healing. Likewise, it is good for your health to accept situations as they are without spending undue time determining blame (which stirs up your stress response and keeps you stuck in the past). Try this phrase: "It is what it is." Then, engage yourself in working to make the situation better.

An advanced form of living from love is practicing commitment to a person or a project or a cause without attachment to the end result being the way "you" want it to be. I say this is advanced because it takes real, conscious intention. When you begin to try this practice, you will quickly learn just how conditional your love can be. We usually offer love or friendship with expectations, or strings attached. Many times, these expectations are unconscious, and they remain unconscious...until they are not met. Then, watch out—our expectations rear their ugly heads, and we end up feeling angry, hurt, betrayed, shocked or any number of negative emotions (stirring up the physiological stress response) that we consequently take out on the person who did not meet our (often unspoken and almost always not agreed-upon) expectations. We are saying, in effect, we are going to do this my way or not at all. It's a recipe for relationship disaster, and it happens all the time. If we can be clear about our expectations at the start, or if we can realize when our own hurt or anger is coming from our own unmet expectations, we can avoid or move quickly through this relational minefield relatively unscathed.

The best way to live, though, is to practice commitment without attachment to the end result, eliminating the minefield altogether. Being committed only when the end result is what I want is a form of pride (not thy will but mine be done). In Buddhist teaching, this kind of attachment leads directly to suffering, and we see that in everyday life. When you can make it your habit to show love to another or offer service to a project in the here-and-now, without requiring or expecting or being attached to the result that this person or project fulfill your needs in a certain way, you will experience a notably greater amount of peace in your life.

Finally, I want to say a word about loving yourself. I strongly encourage you to love yourself enough to live with integrity. I mean, live honestly. Be who you are. Keep your word. Speak the truth. Dishonesty creates internal and external stress that can wreak havoc on your body. I have learned the hard way that you cannot be well when living a lie. There was a time in my life during my depression when I was lying to everyone about an abusive relationship in my life. I thought I was doing it for noble reasons, but regardless of my motive, the lies drove me deeper and deeper into darkness. Before that experience, I thought integrity was key to a healthy life. Now, I know integrity is core. The truth really does set you free—emotionally, mentally, spiritually, relationally and physically—live it.

Breathing Prayer

Connecting with God is called prayer. Countless books have been written on prayer, and it is not my purpose here to add another. Rather, I want to share with you a kind of prayer that you can practice when you hurt so deeply that you cannot speak or when you aren't even sure what to pray. I call it a breathing prayer.

Picture the person—yourself or other(s)—or the current situation that is the focus of your prayer. As you slowly inhale, in your mind simply think or hear yourself saying the word "please." Imagine that you are inhaling the peace of God, and, as it flows through you, imagine God's peace surrounding the person or situation you are picturing. Pause for a moment before you exhale and let yourself feel the sensation of being completely filled with God's love, power, peace, healing, whatever is the focus of your prayer.

As you slowly exhale, release this person or situation fully into God's care while in your mind you think or hear yourself saying the words "thank you." Imagine the person or situation fully healed and happy. Before you inhale, pause for a moment and let yourself experience the sensation of being completely emptied of your concerns.

You can continue this pattern of prayer as you breathe in and out for a short or long period of time. You can change the focus with each breath or after many breaths. You can change the words you say, or you can say no words at all as you let your imagination paint your prayers to God. Let the images be as vivid as you like. Let the feelings of your soul color the canvas in your mind. This simple form of prayer is a way to connect directly with God that transcends language.

If you don't consider yourself a particularly religious person, your practice of this meditative breathing can still help your body move from a fight-or-flight stress response into a state of deep calm. Meditation has been shown to move us from the state of wakeful, rapid brain wave cycles (called beta brain waves) into the state of wakeful relaxation that is so beneficial for our health (called alpha brain waves). Further, studies have linked the practice of meditation to increased activity in the left frontal cortex region of the brain (a region that shows markedly decreased activity in depressed individuals), and the changes in this critical part of our brain are stable over time, meaning the effect of meditation lingers for awhile even after we stop.

For your wellness, I recommend daily prayer. I believe that God is the Source of all life, and we cannot live well when we are disconnected from our Source. If I'm right, breathing prayer will help you live well, and if I'm wrong, breathing prayer will still help you live well. You have nothing to lose but your ongoing stress response, and you have significant health to gain.

❧ 9 ❧

Help, I'm Overwhelmed!
(Getting started, practicing, and getting back on track)

———————

The most common response I get when people learn about lifestyle change for the treatment of depression is hope: there is something I can do to heal! This is immediately followed by a kind of overload: how am I going to incorporate all these practices? After all, I am recommending that you potentially make changes in every single aspect of your life—physical, relational, mental, emotional and spiritual. It's an ambitious undertaking, but I'm confident you can find the motivation. I'm confident because most of the people I know who have struggled with depression, myself included, are willing to do *anything* to escape its relentless, life-sucking, indescribable pain. I practice the 7 Rs as if my life depended on it—because in my experience, it does.

Earlier in this book, I suggested you read <u>The Depression Cure</u> by Dr. Stephen Ilardi. This was not solely to offer you more detailed information on Therapeutic Lifestyle Change, but also for a practical reason. Chapter 10 of that book outlines a step-by-step plan for implementing the initial six Rs over a 12-week period. His book also contains an invaluable troubleshooting guide and tools to track your progress. Dr. Ilardi's work is excellent, and I feel no need to reinvent the wheel, so to speak.

What I want to do is talk about the mind-set you will need for success. You must look at this as a journey on which you are daily practicing the lifestyle choices that will keep you well. Accept that there is no "quick fix," and there is no now-I-am-well-once-and-for-all-and-I-will-be-well-forever-and-always moment in time. Since depression is lifestyle-dependent, we can live in such a way to be well, or we can live in such a way to earn a relapse. It's our choice; we make it day-by-day and moment-by-moment.

On this wellness journey, you can get started by implementing a 12-week program during which you learn healing lifestyle choices. You can address the spiritual choices connected to mental wellness (the seventh R) at any point during this initial program, or you can explore those before or afterwards. If you need assistance with the spiritual dimension of wellness, I encourage you to work with a coach, counselor or religious teacher who understands and supports your spirituality or to read one of the many helpful books available on these topics, some of which are listed in my section on References and Resources at the back of this book.

After that initial 12 weeks, you continue to practice the lifestyle wellness choices you have learned. I know that every day when I awaken, I get to choose a path for my day that will keep me well, or I get to choose a path for my day that will move me closer to darkness and disease. It's that simple. I said "simple," not "easy." Some days, it's anything but easy. Some days, you won't make good choices. Sometimes, life will unexpectedly knock you off track.

In the midst of these times (days, weeks or longer), I find that what works is a return to the basics. My friends in addiction recovery taught me an acronym: H. A. L. T. It stands for Hungry, Angry, Lonely, Tired. Whenever we get too hungry, angry, lonely or tired, we need to halt. We need to stop what we are doing and make a course correction. Even a tiny course correction makes a dramatic, long-term impact.

When I get off track (you need to know that even after a decade of practice, I still go through periods when I get off track in the practice of these lifestyle choices), I intentionally stop and assess each of the 7 Rs in my life. Am I getting enough sleep? Am I feeding myself nutritious foods that support my brain and my body? Am I getting enough bright light? Am I exercising? Am I spending time with life-giving people, limiting time with toxic people and giving myself in service to something bigger than my self? Am I managing my mind? Am I connecting with God and dwelling in gratitude and love? Is there anyone I need to forgive?

Next, I prioritize my time in such a way that I reincorporate the practice(s) I have been missing. I literally schedule my lifestyle choices on my calendar. I find that until something has time and space assigned to it, it's not really a commitment in my world. I renew my own radical dedication to my wellness. I do it intentionally, powerfully and without apology because I have learned that no one else can do it for me. No one else has as much at stake.

When I need it, I seek help from a friend, coach, counselor or health professional, and I don't keep myself stuck by spending undue time beating myself up for getting off track in the first place—not helpful. The longer a practice has slipped, the longer it can take me to work it back into my life. That's okay. As I said before, this is a journey; I have the rest of my life to practice, so do you. Some days, the best we can do is to make it through the day—just merely survive—and that's enough. The gift is that we get a "restart" at each day's end, and each morning brings us a new chance to practice. There is no point on your journey when it is ever too late to begin living well.

❧ 10 ❧

A Word About Meds

As you have been reading this book about using lifestyle choices to help heal depression, you may have wondered how I feel about psychotropic drugs. Let me be clear: I am <u>not</u> anti-medication. I would probably not be alive today without it! I simply understand that medication has limits as well as side effects that can be quite challenging.

I have a friend who has worked in the field of community mental health for years. She helps diagnose and recommend treatment strategies for people who struggle with chronic, disabling brain diseases like bipolar disorder and schizophrenia as well as people who, due to factors beyond their control, cannot implement every lifestyle change that helps heal depression. She reminds me that for many, mental illness is a lifelong battle.

A lot of these folks have tried countless hours of exercise, supplementation, therapy, self-help, even exorcisms, and they continue to struggle. For them, psychotropic medication is not an option; it is a necessity. Many of these people have been shamed and hurt by well-meaning family members, friends, holistic practitioners and the religious community. I want to acknowledge the complexity of their situation and offer support and acceptance. I believe that in some cases it is good, even honorable, to take meds for the rest of your life in order to cope with your illness.

I am not a doctor, and I am not qualified to offer advice regarding the use of these substances in any particular case. I encourage you to check with your own healthcare provider to determine what course of treatment is best for you. Whether you take medication for depression or not, incorporating healthy lifestyle practices into your daily routine is an excellent way for you to support your ongoing brain health.

❧ 11 ❧

Hope

Those who study the human energy field might find it an intriguing exercise to consider connections between my 7 Rs and the seven traditional chakras of Eastern medicine. While I am not such an expert, I am nonetheless able to appreciate the way different cultures in different geographical regions across different time periods have found ways to organize their understanding of what our bodies need for health in ways that have striking similarities. Humans are humans wherever you go and whenever you live, and what makes us well in one time and one culture tends to also make us well in another. This knowledge gives me hope for all of us.

At Brookhaven, I was taught a definition of "hope" that I like very much: HOPE is the feeling you have that the feeling you have won't last forever. Hope is what I want my book to convey to all of those suffering from clinical depression and to all of those who love them—the feeling you have won't last forever. You can laugh again. You can know joy. Don't give up.

In the face of the epidemic of clinical depression in our world, my stand is that we create an outbreak of mental wellness that will spread across the globe so thoroughly that depression is no longer a leading cause of disability and suffering on our planet. As the vast majority of depression is lifestyle-dependent, we CAN help heal this. Wherever you live today, join me in spreading the word about these lifestyle choices to everyone you know. Practice these 7 Rs, and support your lifetime mental wellness.

Epilogue

At the time, clinical depression felt to me like one long mind rape, a devastating force that assaulted my brain, hurting me and controlling me against my will, a loss of power over my very thoughts, perceptions, intellect, emotions, imagination, even my memories. Depression broke my body, my mind and my soul. I never want to endure it again, and I would never wish that experience on another human being.

Yet unexpectedly, I am tremendously grateful for my experience. I have been transformed by my encounter with this darkness. I have wisdom and strength and grace and hope and understanding and joy that were not available to me before. I know myself much more deeply. I am expanded and defined in ways that were previously beyond my imagination.

Today, I am rich with the hard-won wisdom that only comes from facing your own darkness and seeing others clearly in theirs. I am rich with the strength of overcoming my depression and reclaiming my life. I am rich with the compassion of one who is humbled by her own failures. I am rich with the mercy of one who found love and acceptance in the most unlikely of places and in spite of herself.

As I interact with the people God puts in my life, I realize that I needed to know depression. I needed to know anxiety. I needed to know a desperate longing for death. I needed to know the hellish prison of abuse. I needed to know Roxanne who failed, Roxanne the liar, Roxanne the adulterer, Roxanne who was not a good mother, not a good wife, not a good friend, not a good pastor. I needed to know Roxanne who couldn't figure it all out and couldn't fix it, broken and weak and incompetent and needy and hopeless. I needed to let go of my arrogance and my sense of entitlement. I needed to know what it was like to be absolutely lost. I needed to know Superwoman, defeated, with the last of her proud rope tied in a noose around her own slender neck.

And because I know all those things, because I know them in every cell of my body and in the deepest recesses of my soul, I also firmly know that there is nowhere you can go where God will not pursue you and love you and pull you back toward life. I know that there is nothing you can do that will separate you from the love of the One who created you. I know that there absolutely is a way to heal.

Because I once dwelled in darkness, I know the way out. May this book help guide you to light. It is my great honor to walk beside you on the journey.

Roxanne Reneé
Kansas City, Missouri, U.S.A.
October 2010

Postscript

January 5, 2001

As I was driving today with the boys, I reached down to turn on the radio, then I stopped. I stopped and simply listened because I realized that the most exquisite music in the whole wide world is the sound of their two voices, laughing and talking back and forth with one another in the back seat of my car.

Thank you, God, that you did not grant my desperate prayers for death. Thank you for these precious angels. Thank you that I get to share life with them. Thank you. Thank you. Thank you...

Laughing Again - Roxanne Reneé

Appendix A

Symptoms of Clinical Depression

- Difficulty concentrating, remembering things or making decisions
- Fatigue, loss of energy, feeling tired all the time
- Feeling guilty, hopeless, worthless or helpless
- Loss of pleasure or interest in activities once enjoyed, including sex
- Persistent physical symptoms that do not respond to treatment, such as chronic pain or digestive disorders that do not go away
- Persistent sad, anxious or "empty" mood
- Reduced appetite and weight loss OR increased appetite and weight gain
- Restlessness, irritability
- Sleeping too much, or being unable to go to sleep or to stay asleep
- Thoughts of death or suicide or making suicide attempts

If you experience five or more of these symptoms for two weeks or longer, or if the symptoms are severe, you could have clinical depression. Consult your health care professional right away. Clinical depression is one of the most treatable mental illnesses.

Appendix B

Let All Mortal Flesh Keep Silence

An ancient chant of devotion based on Habakkuk 2:20
"Let all the earth keep silence before Him"

Translated from the Greek by Gerard Moultrie
Arranged by Ralph Vaughan Williams to the
French medieval folk melody, "Picardy"

Let all mortal flesh keep silence,
And with fear and trembling stand;
Ponder nothing earthly minded,
For with blessing in His hand,
Christ our God to earth descendeth,
Our full homage to demand.

Rank on rank the host of heaven
Spreads its vanguard on the way,
As the Light of light descendeth
From the realms of endless day,
That the powers of hell may vanish
As the darkness clears away.

At His feet the six-winged seraph,
Cherubim with sleepless eye,
Veil their faces to the presence,
As with ceaseless voice they cry:
Alleluia, Alleluia
Alleluia, Lord Most High!

Laughing Again - Roxanne Reneé

Appendix C

It's Not Christmas (in my Broken Heart)

In our society, depression peaks during the winter months. For those who are suffering, the holidays are an intensely painful time. The juxtaposition of everyone else's effervescent happiness and your own deep sadness is excruciating. I wrote this song in 2005 in an attempt to capture the way it felt to be contemplating suicide during the Christmas season of 2000.

© Copyright 2005
Words and Music by Roxanne Reneé
Arranged by Kerry Karr and Roxanne Reneé

VERSE 1:

   G

I'm way past lonely, way past grief

  Am   D2   D

In silent desperation, I seek only relief

       C

Some days I don't get out of bed, just lie in misery

       G   D2   C2

I'm a stranger now, a danger now to me

       G   D2   C2

VERSE 2:

   G

Another sunny day begins outside this place

    Am   D2   D

But it stops right at the threshold, can't touch my face

    C

And though there's tinsel hangin' on these walls and a
Christmas tree

    G   D2   C2

Hope's blocked away, locked away from me

CHORUS:

      C   G

It's a silent night, but not a holy night

    Am   D

My heart has no faith to sing, no gift to bring

      C   G C

This winter holiday won't fix me an-y-way

    G   C   Am

I'll step out before the music starts

          G   D   C

'Cause it's not Christmas in my broken heart

VERSE 3:

    G

In deepest fear and darkness, Life clings tenaciously

   Am   D2   D

And forces me to see the truth that I don't want to see

    C

That for blessing or for cursing I'm gonna leave a legacy:

   G   D2   C2

Hope spoken, or lives broken, due to me

CHORUS:

       C   G

It's a silent night, but not a holy night

        Am   D

My heart has no faith to sing, no gift to bring

           C   G   C

This winter holiday won't fix me an-y-way

      G   C   Am

I'll step out before the music starts

               G   D   C

'Cause it's not Christmas in my broken heart

BRIDGE:

Em   Em

Thoughts inside my head (give up)...Like "You're already dead" (give up)

         C   D2 D

Like "There's no getting up from this far below" (give up...give up)

        Em   Em

While those who love me say (stay)..."There's gotta be another way" (stay...stay!)

  Am   D2   D

But I can't feel the love they try to show

FINAL CHORUS:

N/C   C   C

Damn...this...silent night,

                  G   G

 I need Your holy light

            Am   Am

My heart has no faith to sing,

            D2   D

No gift to bring

[Instrumental interlude / vocal ad lib]

    C   C   G   G   Am   Am   D2   D   //

                    C   G   C

...Could this holy day reach me an-y-way?

            G   C   Am

I'll stay here and let the music start

                      G   D   C

Though it's not Christmas in my bro-ken heart

TAG:

                          G   D   Am7   G

No, it's not Christmas in my bro-   ken   heart

References and Resources

For readability, I chose not to cite sources within my text. The purpose of a footnote or an endnote is to give credit where credit is due and to guide the reader toward further reading and research. For places in my text where I clearly acknowledged my source and listed enough information on a given topic that you can simply Google the name or subject matter for further research, I have not provided information here. Rather, what I have chosen to share in this section is a list of resources that I have found helpful in my ongoing research and in my personal journey to live well.

Books

For a more in-depth and scientific look at the first 6 Rs, a step-by-step guide for implementing Therapeutic Lifestyle Change and an extensive bibliography, read <u>The Depression Cure: The 6-Step Program to Beat Depression without Drugs</u> by Stephen S. Ilardi, PhD.

For excellent information on your brain and how to care for it, read <u>Making a Good Brain Great</u> by Daniel G. Amen, MD.

For detailed information on the chemicals of emotion, read <u>Molecules of Emotion: The Science Behind Mind-Body Medicine</u> by Candace B. Pert, PhD.

For engaging information on your body as a whole, read <u>You Staying Young: The Owner's Manual for Extending Your Warranty</u> by Michael F. Roizen, MD and Mehmet Oz, MD.

For increasing your personal organization and efficiency, thus allowing your brain the clarity you need to relax, read <u>Getting Things Done: The Art of Stress-Free Productivity</u> by David Allen.

For a new perspective on your problems that can free you from suffering, read Byron Katie's <u>Loving What Is</u>.

For help overcoming mental roadblocks to wellness, read <u>Why People Don't Heal and How They Can</u> by Caroline Myss, PhD.

For a list of helpful affirmations, organized according to type and physical area of disease, read Louise L. Hay's <u>You Can Heal Your Life</u> and/or <u>Heal Your Body</u>.

For practical techniques to overcome lifelong patterns of thinking and behavior that have kept you stuck, read <u>Reinventing Your Life: The Breakthrough Program to End Negative Behavior and Feel Great Again</u> by Jeffrey E. Young, PhD and Janet S. Klosko, PhD.

For inspiration to celebrate life, even in the face of impending death, read <u>The Last Lecture</u> by Randy Pausch, PhD.

For invaluable guidance for women that connects body, mind, spirit and life, read <u>Women's Bodies, Women's Wisdom</u> by Christiane Northrup, MD.

For honest prayers, written and compiled by women to reveal, nurture and celebrate all the seasons of life, read <u>WomenPsalms</u> from Saint Mary's Press/Christian Brothers Publications and <u>Women's Uncommon Prayers</u> from Morehouse Publishing.

For a guide to soulful living that offers a symbolic look at life's journey, read Thomas Moore's classic work, <u>Care of the Soul</u>.

For a fresh look at authentic Christianity, read <u>Messy Spirituality</u> by Michael Yaconelli.

For help with some toxic religious beliefs, read <u>12 "Christian" Beliefs That Can Drive You Crazy: Relief From False Assumptions</u> by Henry Cloud, PhD and John Townsend, PhD.

For those struggling with the reality of pain and evil alongside their belief in a loving God, read William P. Young's <u>The Shack</u>.

For those navigating deep grief, read Rev. John Claypool's personal and very honest book, <u>Tracks of a Fellow Struggler</u>.

For those who want a Biblical 12-step program, read <u>The Twelve Steps, A Spiritual Journey: A Working Guide for Healing Damaged Emotions</u>.

For a truly thought-provoking, often wry and ironic, look at spiritual topics, read Rev. Frederick Buechner's <u>Wishful Thinking: A Seeker's ABC</u> and <u>Whistling in the Dark: A Doubter's Dictionary</u>.

For a profound, adventurous, funny and moving chronicle of one woman's journey to heal her life and claim her own truth, read <u>Eat, Pray, Love</u> by Elizabeth Gilbert.

For refreshingly honest, irreverently reverent reflections on faith and life, read Anne Lamott's <u>Traveling Mercies: Some Thoughts on Faith</u>, <u>Plan B: Further Thoughts on Faith</u>, and <u>Operating Instructions: A Journal of My Son's First Year.</u>

Products

Guidance of experts in naturopathic and functional medicine who offer personal, phone call and video call consultations with ongoing support and top-quality supplements
<u>www.kcwellnessdimensions.com</u>

Light boxes
<u>www.caribbeansunbox.com</u> or
<u>www.lighttherapyproducts.com</u>

Low-cost supplements www.vitacost.com

Target heart rate: learn how to find yours, and get support for walking www.thewalkingsite.com/thr

YoGo™ workout DVD by Happy Mind, LLC provides a yoga warm up, yoga cool down, 25 minutes of aerobic cardio workout and 25 minutes of core strengthening workout along with positive support for mental wellness from Candace Vanice and Roxanne Reneé.
www.yogoworkout.com

Websites

Brookhaven Hospital
www.brookhavenhospital.com

Crazy Meds! The Good, The Bad & The Funny
of Neurological Medications
www.crazymeds.us

Depression and Bipolar Support Alliance
www.dbsalliance.org

Landmark Education
www.landmarkeducation.com

National Domestic Violence Hotline
www.thehotline.org

National Institute of Mental Health

www.nimh.nih.gov

Roxanne Reneé

www.roxannerenee.com

Suicide Hotlines by State

www.suicidehotlines.com

Therapeutic Lifestyle Change

www.psych.ku.edu/tlc

World Health Organization

www.who.int/mental_health/management

Acknowledgements

My most heartfelt gratitude forever goes to those who fought for my life, quite simply refusing to let me die. If anything I do touches another life with hope or blessing, please know that YOU made it possible. When I could not feel God, you were God's voice and hands and eyes and ears and arms and heart. You carried me. Thank you Doty & Randy, Judy & John, Pam & Dave, Nancy & Wayne, Loretta & Murl, Karen L, Susan M, Verna, Shari, Kasey & Jim, Susan L, James, Mitzi, Joanie, Sally, Jeanie, Lucille & Warner, Amy M, June, Scott P, Cat S, Kris D, Darrell S, Tim T, Martha, Sandy and my Dad for giving me the most tenacious love I've ever known.

My beloved Truman and Jay, thank you for bringing me joy every single day. Being your mom is my greatest adventure and my highest honor. You were my reason to persevere and, ultimately, to win.

Thank you Mom & Waymond, Amy & family, Margie & Bill, Kenny & family and Christina & Paul. Without you, I'm not "me." I love you.

For praying me through the long, dark night, thank you to the people of God at Englewood Baptist Church in Kansas City, Pleasant Valley Baptist Church Support Group Ministries in Liberty, Pryor Resources, Inc. in Overland Park, First Christian Church in North Kansas

City, Central Seminary in Shawnee, Chandler Baptist Church in Liberty, Midwestern Seminary in Kansas City, William Jewell College in Liberty and First Baptist Church in Joplin.

For compassionate, professional care, thank you to Stephen Samuelson, MD; Karladine Graves, DO; Jerry Brown, PhD, LPC; Jude LaClaire, PhD; Lisa Everett FACA, CCN; Regina O'Brien LPC; Mary Linda Hughes LPC, NCC and Rev. Betty-Jo Anderson as well as the staff at Research Psychiatric Center in Kansas City, St. Luke's Northland Hospital in Smithville and Brookhaven Hospital in Tulsa.

David Sexton, thank you for being my legal champion when I did not have a voice.

Leslie & Glenn, Albert, Brian R, Tac, Cat N, Jim O, Kerry, Kellie, Cindi, Michelle A, Margaret & John, Karen H, Amanda, Karen O, Matthew, Steve, Scott H, Greg, Ian, Tiffany & Chris, Kathy, the people of God at North Star UMC, Terry R, Alana, Caroline, Annie, Jody, Lynn, Marcia, Jenny, Sandy & Steve, Jeff R, Michelle R, Pam, Kelly, Shannon, Strick, Kristin B and Curtis, thank you for friendship, for believing in the value of my story and for encouraging me to tell it.

Thank you to Dr. Corey Priest for friendship that goes the distance, for brilliant nutritional guidance and for functional medicine that keeps my family well. When I appear nutritionally savvy, it's because I have listened to you.

Acknowledgements

Mary Linda Hughes, professional counselor and really wise woman, thank you for ongoing emotional and mental support, sage guidance, creative problem-solving, unfailing honesty and consistent gentleness. Your space is a sanctuary where I can rage against injustice, cry my heart out and then discern a plan to overcome.

Thank you to Dr. Steve Timmer for excellent chiropractic care for my sons and myself; your skill helps my nervous system run smoothly in spite of occasional mishaps involving heavy furniture!

Julie Worden, personal trainer extraordinaire, thank you for coaching me through yoga, for helping me unravel my food addiction and for teaching me a better way to eat and live.

Thank you to the professional colleagues who have reviewed and endorsed my work, especially Stephen Ilardi, PhD; Michael Brown, ND; Farrel Douglas, MD; Sally King, LCSW, LSCSW; Richard Ortiz, MD; and Stephanie Revels, MD. It is my great honor to know you and to work alongside you promoting wellness.

Thank you to Evan & Rick for inspiring me, for loyal friendship and for introducing me to Landmark Education. Who I am is the possibility of liberation!

Lauren, you were there when I first birthed the 7 Rs. Thank you for your authentic friendship on this sacred journey.

Thank you to my sister, Amy, for home-cooked meals,

practical support and continuing to call me forward in the face of confusing and painful obstacles. I hope you're right about those jewels.

Laura, my cousin and co-conspirator in creating health and joy, thank you for lunch talks, long walks, weekend retreats and your unfailing belief in me.

Thank you to Josh for fiercely loyal friendship, for helping me to see things more clearly, for pushing me to keep going even when it hurts and for helping me laugh in spite of my tears.

Joseph Ward, channel of God's healing and light and wisdom, thank you for playing the music of my soul.

Thank you to Mark Allen, Julie Anderson, Donovan Dodrill and Tim Marks. You fight every day for what is right, and I am honored to have you on my legal team.

Duncan McCloud, my MacBook Pro, thank you for consistent superior functioning, for intuitive, friendly ease of use and for being my daily partner in creative work. Yes, my computer has a name, and I am thankful for him every day. If you own a Mac, you understand.

Eric, brilliant business coach, marketing strategist, tech guru, graphic designer par excellence and entre-prenurial partner, thank you not only for your outstanding work but also for your incomparable friendship. God blesses me through you.

Thank you to my weekly prayer group—Diane, Laurie,

Leslie, Linda, Lisa, Michelle and Tricia. For five years now, we've kept each other centered, safe and sane. You are my soul sisters, and you bless my life every single day. No matter where the journey leads, I am honored to go with you on the way.

Doty, my very best friend for over two decades, you braved the vilest darkness and risked your own life to save mine. You consistently call forth my best self, sometimes before it even exists. I treasure the haven of our friendship...fully safe, fully known, fully loved. From the depths of my soul, I thank you.

Yea, though I walk through the valley of the shadow of death, thou art with me. My God, when I was stuck in hell, you pursued me even there. Thank you for love that will not let me go.

About the Author

Roxanne Reneé, a nationally-acclaimed trainer and motivational speaker, specializes in the interconnection between body, mind, heart and soul. In her private practice, Roxanne offers personalized therapeutic coaching to individuals and groups. She is in demand as a dynamic trainer and workshop leader. As the featured wellness expert on the YoGo™ fitness DVD, Roxanne brings practical lifestyle wellness training into countless homes every day. Roxanne holds a Master of Divinity degree with a focus in Pastoral Care and Counseling. She is a licensed and ordained minister, and she currently serves at a church in the greater Kansas City area. You may contact Roxanne at www.RoxanneRenee.com.